TO BRIE
OR NOT
TO BRIE...

BETER
GRATE
THAN
NEVER

 Gouda morning to you!

YOU GOTTA FIGHT
FOR YOUR RIGHT
TO HAVAAAARRRTII!!

SWEET DREAMS ARE MADE OF CHEESE;
WHO AM I TO DIS A BRIE
SWEET DREAMS ARE MADE OF CHEESE;
SOME OF THEM ARE BLUE AND BRIE

HAVARTI LIKE IT'S 1999!

GRILLED CHEESE

KITCHEN

GRILLED CHEESE

KITCHEN

BREAD + CHEESE + EVERYTHING
IN BETWEEN

Heidi Gibson with Nate Pollak

photographs BY ANTONIS ACHILLEOS

CHRONICLE BOOKS
SAN FRANCISCO

Library of Congress Cataloging-in-Publication Data available.
ISBN 978-1-4521-4459-7

Manufactured in China

MIX
Paper from responsible sources
FSC™ C008047
FSC
www.fsc.org

Designed by **VANESSA DINA**
Typesetting by **FRANK BRAYTON**

10 9 8

Chronicle Books LLC
680 Second Street
San Francisco, California 94107
www.chroniclebooks.com

CONTENTS

Preface 10

Grilled Cheese Is Magical, Grilled Cheese Is Love

Introduction 12

What Makes a Great Grilled Cheese?

BREAKFAST 20

Classic Breakfast Grilled Cheese **23**

Breakfast-in-Bed Grilled Cheese **24**

Breakfast Popper Grilled Cheese **25**

Farmer's Breakfast Grilled Cheese **26**

Breakfast Piglet Grilled Cheese **28**

Green Eggs and Ham Grilled Cheese **29**

Huevos Rollando Grilled Cheese **30**

Sunday Brunch Grilled Cheese **32**

GRILLED CHEESE SANDWICHES 36

Mousetrap Grilled Cheese **38**

Basque Sheep Grilled Cheese **40**

Mac 'n' Cheese Grilled Cheese **42**

Ultimate California Grilled Cheese **45**

Mushroom-Gruyère Grilled Cheese **46**

Moscone Grilled Cheese **48**

Feta Fetish Grilled Cheese 50

Black Bean and Fresh Corn Grilled Cheese 52

The Catch Grilled Cheese 55

Foghorn Leghorn Grilled Cheese 56

Moroccan Chicken Grilled Cheese 58

Indian Leftovers Grilled Cheese 60

Bro 'Wich Project Grilled Cheese 61

Club Turkey Grilled Cheese 64

Wild Turkey Grilled Cheese 65

Thanksgiving Leftovers Grilled Cheese 66

Jalapeño Popper Grilled Cheese 68

Piglet Grilled Cheese 69

Hawaiian Grilled Cheese 71

Cubano Grilled Cheese 72

Truffled Grilled Cheese with Bacon and Chives 75

Butternut Buster Grilled Cheese 76

Don Gondola Grilled Cheese 78

Pizza-wich Grilled Cheese 79

Muffaletta Grilled Cheese 81

Roast Beef and Blue Cheese Grilled Cheese 83

Windy City Grilled Cheese 84

American Dip Grilled Cheese 85

St. Patrick's Day Grilled Cheese 86

Reubenesque Grilled Cheese 89

Grilled Cheese Birthday Cake 90

SOUP 94

Ten-Minute Tomato Soup 97

Broccoli-Cheddar Soup 98

Kale and Potato Soup 99

Baked Potato Soup 100

Celery Purée Soup 102

Luscious Mushroom Soup 103

Fresh Corn Chowder 105

Curry-Cauliflower Soup 107

Butternut Squash Soup 108

Spiced Coconut-Carrot Soup 110

Split Pea Soup 111

Smoky Lentil Soup 113

White Bean and Ham Soup 114

Pulled Pork Stew 115

American Chili 116

MAC 'N' CHEESE 118

Basic Mac 'n' Cheese 120

Gruyère, Garlic, and White Wine Mac 124

Fontina, Mushroom, and Thyme Mac 126

Mozzarella, Pesto, and Tomato Mac 128

Crab Mac 130

BBQ Chicken Mac 132

Ham and Herb Mac 134

Asiago, Prosciutto, and Sage Mac **136**

Bacon and Jalapeño Mac **138**

Chili Mac **141**

PICKLES, SPREADS,
 AND SIDES 144

Bread 'n' Butter Pickles **147**

Giardiniera **149**

Pickled Red Onions **151**

Sweet Pickled Jalapeños **152**

Preserved Meyer Lemons **153**

Cranberry Sauce **154**

Apricot-Jalapeño Relish **155**

Kalamata Tapenade **156**

Muffaletta Olive Salad **157**

Moroccan Green Olive, Artichoke, and
Preserved Lemon Spread **158**

Basil-Lavender Pesto **159**

Apple Mustard **160**

Balsamic Onion Marmalade **161**

Kale Slaw **163**

Glossary 164

Sources 168

Acknowledgments 169

Index 170

GRILLED CHEESE IS MAGICAL, GRILLED CHEESE IS LOVE

Nate and I first started to research, plan, and develop The American Grilled Cheese Kitchen in the winter of 2009. It was the height of the Great Recession, and the idea of two industry amateurs opening up an artisanal, gourmet grilled cheese restaurant was simply outrageous—to our friends, to our family, even to us.

Thirty-five banks didn't believe in us. Industry professionals didn't believe in us. We even doubted ourselves. But grilled cheese—cheese toastie, toasted cheese, Welsh rarebit, *croque monsieur* . . . whatever you call it—is something you *have* to believe in. Something wonderful happens when you melt cheese between two pieces of buttered bread. The sight and the smell universally evoke smiles; it's magical. Everyone can relate to it, everyone can feel it, everyone can love it. Really, somehow, grilled cheese is a culinary miracle that has the power to elicit everything from nostalgic moments from childhood and the laid-back years of early adulthood to the savory satisfaction of being an adult who can eat grilled cheese anytime you want to.

We believed, and continue to believe, in grilled cheese. It inspired us to create and grow a successful restaurant concept that served more than a million people in our community in less than four years. But most important, it brought Nate and me together.

We met in an elevator in an office building in downtown San Francisco in 2007. I had been working at software companies for over a decade. Nate had been billing hours as an analyst for a strategy consulting firm for almost as long. We were not professional cooks. We were not restaurant managers. We were driven professionals.

Yet we still had as much fun as possible. I spent my weekends participating in grilled cheese competitions—I have seven trophies from national contests, displayed proudly in our first restaurant—and riding my bicycle across California. Nate competed in chili cook-offs and played accordion professionally in a polka-party band

around town. We had an appetite for fun and adrenaline. This served us well as we built our relationship and, in the near future, our business.

As fate would have it, we (us and a lot of the country!) were laid off from our office jobs in December of 2008, after failed mortgage–backed securities took down the global economy. Afterward, we spent a good amount of time thinking about our next steps: scheming and brainstorming fun businesses that we could own and operate, together.

One Saturday afternoon during that time, I brought home my fifth grilled cheese trophy from a regional competition. After a few drinks and a small celebration, Nate took out a pen and paper and we started planning what would become The American Grilled Cheese Kitchen. We soon found we had complementary skills. I had natural cooking and kitchen instincts, good knowledge of food and cheese, and a unique scientific approach to testing and creating delicious grilled cheese sandwiches. Nate loved developing the restaurant concept and our brand, thinking through the entire customer experience, and handling all aspects of administrative business management, from finance to marketing and HR to technology. We divided and conquered.

For a couple with no income, we spent heaps of our scarce cash on fine groceries and specialty foods so we could develop and test our recipes. We studied hundreds of cookbooks, took endless small-business planning classes, and exhausted every professional networking opportunity that might help us. We dined out when we had the chance, sneaking notepads under the tables to document what we liked/didn't like/were going to copy for our restaurant.

We ate grilled cheese for breakfast, lunch, and dinner, and sometimes for dessert. We tested our baked treats, soups, salads, coffees, and beers with friends and at dinner parties. Everyone's opinion mattered to us; every data point was valuable. The coffee-and-cookie tasting party was particularly memorable: After ten kinds of coffee and twelve types of cookies, most of the guests were hovering off the ground from the sugar and caffeine overload.

We completed a seventy-page business plan and secured a brick-and-mortar restaurant space in San Francisco. After being denied capital from multiple sources, we drained the remainder of our savings and our retirement accounts to fund the construction and opening of the first American Grilled Cheese Kitchen.

When you believe in magic, you throw caution to the wind; and we believed in grilled cheese.

Saying it was hard work is an understatement; we were on a shoestring budget and enlisted friends to help with drywall and painting, traded with artists to help with decorations, and lived off of ingredient samples while we developed the menu. Blood, sweat, tears, and LOTS of bread, butter, and cheese (and the occasional beer) is what went into the opening of our first store. But Nate and I, and our supporting cast, were united in serving a common mission, which we by then had defined: To serve the tastiest grilled cheese sandwiches using the highest-quality local and unique ingredients with the best possible service.

And that's what we did.

We opened the first American Grilled Cheese Kitchen in May of 2010. I was the culinary director and champion grilled-cheese maker, with the official title "Commander in Cheese." Nate oversaw all business operations, earning the title "The Big Cheese." The store was a smash success. We had no experience, but we had no fear. We learned everything as fast as we could and constantly strived for improvement. People lined up around the block to try our grilled cheese and smoky tomato soup, and to enjoy the Kitchen experience. Almost five years later, after dozens of menu revisions, expanded catering services, a close-to-fifty-person staff, three restaurants and more on the way, and now a cookbook, our wonderful customers continue to line up and support our mission. They continue to enjoy the magic of our grilled cheese and comfort foods. It's been the most fulfilling

and gratifying experience of our lives. There's nothing like the anticipation, the satisfaction of making one of our toasty, melty, buttery grilled cheese sandwiches for a customer and ultimately the smile earned after he or she bites into it. In many cases, these customers have become our friends—we host their wedding and birthday parties, make their child's first grilled cheese, and bring treats to their dogs that are waiting on our patio. And we are grateful every day for their loyalty and support.

In 2013, we opened our second location in San Francisco, a larger facility allowing us to expand our menu beyond our grilled cheeses, soups, salads, and baked treats. With additional kitchen facilities, we developed recipes for some classic comfort food dishes like buttermilk fried chicken and a B.E.L.T. sandwich (bacon, fried egg, lettuce, tomato, and Tapatío aioli, a house specialty). We also developed slow-roasted meat recipes, like our coffee-rubbed pulled pork, which became excellent ingredients for grilled cheese sandwiches, mac 'n' cheeses, soups, and other menu items.

The third outpost opened in 2015, and Team American, as we like to refer to ourselves, plans to open additional stores in San Francisco and the greater Bay Area.

If you can open a business, especially a restaurant, with the person you love most in the world, there is definitely magic there. Nate and I continue to complement each other, in work, in friendship, and in life. We got married in 2014 and live in San Francisco with our awesome rescue dogs, McLovin (Mickey) and Tillamook (Tilly). We're so excited to share our recipes with you. What a thrill! We've had so much fun with these recipes and we really hope you do too.

And yes, we still eat grilled cheese almost every day.

With much hot, cheesy love,

Heidi and Nate

WHAT MAKES A GREAT GRILLED CHEESE?

We get this question almost every day. There are a few simple rules—okay, suggestions—for crafting delicious grilled cheeses.

USE GREAT INGREDIENTS

This one may sound obvious, but it's the most important place to start. Use the best-tasting artisan bread you can get your hands on, choose cheeses that you'd want to eat on a cheese plate, and select fresh, ripe, high-quality ingredients for the fillings and add-ons. A really good seasonal tomato fresh out of the garden or from the farmers' market will taste better in any recipe than a mealy out-of-season tomato with no flavor, and that's true in a grilled cheese as much as anywhere. And don't cut corners on the "secondary" ingredients either—use good-quality fresh butter or extra-virgin olive oil to create that perfect crunchy crust—the flavor will shine through. There are very few ingredients in most grilled cheese sandwiches, so make every one count.

Bread

What's the most important part of a good grilled cheese, the bread or the cheese? Our opinion, though some may consider it heresy, is that the bread wins this showdown. Our go-to bread is a *pain au levain* (country-style French bread made with partial whole-wheat flour and natural fermentation, shaped into *batards*, or oval loaves) made a few blocks from our first restaurant at Pinkie's Bakery. Pinkie's levain is a wonder to behold, slightly sour with great structure and a bit of tooth, crackling crust, and just the right touch of salt. Prowl your local small bakeries and find the gems made in your own neighborhood. For a great grilled cheese, the bread is best when it's not perfectly fresh, so get a loaf of your favorite bread for dinner and make an outstanding sandwich with the remainder the next day. Buy unsliced loaves to cut yourself or have the bakery slice it to your specification, if you can; you want slices approximately ½ in [12 mm] thick for the optimal bread-to-cheese ratio.

Generally, you want to look for breads with a dense crumb and some chewiness to them; these breads will hold up best to buttering and toasting, plus will be more durable if you have any wet ingredients like tomatoes or onions. Be careful when you use bread

with some sugar, like honey whole-wheat or Hawaiian bread; the sugar will cause the bread to brown faster, so you will need to be on guard for burning.

Our favorite breads for grilled cheese are listed below, and you can find descriptions of the breads in the Glossary on page 164:

9-grain/multigrain	Pretzel rolls/bread
Brioche	Pumpernickel
Challah	Rye, including light, dark, and marble rye
Focaccia	
Italian loaf	Semolina
Miche	Sourdough
Oat bread	Whole-wheat/stone-ground wheat/honey whole-wheat
Pain au levain	
Pain de mie	

Butter

You can use salted or unsalted butter, compound butter (which is just a fancy name for butter with flavoring added in, such as garlic or herbs), margarine, olive oil, or even mayonnaise and it's still a grilled cheese sandwich. There is a dizzying array of butter options on the market today: cultured, European-style, whipped, light, churned, ghee, even goat butter. We encourage you to try different alternatives and see the effect they have on the sandwich, but we prefer high-quality regular sweet cream (uncultured) salted butter as our go-to standard for grilled cheese. Some purists will insist on European butter or ghee, which have higher fat-to-water ratios and are more expensive, but we find that we can't tell the difference in the finished sandwich, and sweet cream butter is more readily available. Salt content can vary widely among salted butters, but not so much that you'll be able to tell the difference in a grilled cheese.

We use butter at room temperature so that it is easy to spread but does not soak into the bread. Our goal is a light crispy crunch just on the outside of the bread, so we butter just the side of the bread that will come in contact with the hot skillet, and we use butter very sparingly. Spread the butter with a butter or table knife, as thinly as you can. Don't worry about trying to get the butter evenly spread across every corner; the butter will melt in the pan and take care of the edges. We prefer to butter the bread rather than melt the butter in the pan and then place the bread on top. That way the butter is less likely to burn, will be more evenly distributed, and will be less likely to soak into the bread, yielding a more evenly crunchy crust.

We store our butter in the refrigerator and take out the amount we need about an hour before we'll be using it. Just cut a chunk of butter off the stick and let it come to room temperature in a small dish. If you don't have time to wait for your butter to soften, warm it in the microwave, checking every 5 seconds, until soft but not melted. If you accidentally heat it too much and it's begun to melt, place the dish back in the fridge while you get your other ingredients ready and it should firm up a bit quickly.

Usually it won't matter which side of the bread you deem to be the outside, but if you are using slices from a *boule* or *batard,* one side of the bread is likely to be a bit smaller than the other side. Butter the smaller side and you'll have a neater-looking sandwich.

Cheese
Now that we've discussed the bread and butter, we can't leave the cheese hanging. There are no hard-and-fast rules, but in general the best cheeses for grilled cheese are "semisoft" and "semihard" cheeses. We do use a couple of hard cheeses (e.g., Idiazábal, a smoked, aged sheep's-milk cheese from Spain, and Parmesan), but they are usually grated and used sparingly for flavor because they don't melt as beautifully as the semisoft and semihard. We also use some soft cheeses (e.g., chèvre and Brie), but they are very much the exception. We pair hard or soft cheeses with a good melting cheese to get that grilled cheese ooey-gooeyness.

There are great melting cheeses from all over the world, made with every kind of milk—cow, goat, sheep, and water buffalo. If you are slicing the cheese yourself, try to slice the semisoft and semihard cheeses about ⅛ in [3 mm] thick. (Cheese is easier to slice when cold.) Hard cheeses can be grated, or sliced very thinly, to facilitate melting. For simplicity's sake, we call for "slices" of cheese in the ingredient lists, although we realize that not all cheese chunks are conveniently shaped to match a bread slice. For our purposes, one "slice" means enough to just about cover the surface of the bread in a ⅛-in [3-mm] layer, and should weigh about ¾ oz [20 g].

Here is a list of good melting cheeses you can explore as you craft your own grilled cheese masterpieces.

Asiago

Bel Paese

Blue

Brick

Brie

Butterkäse

Cantal

Cheddar, white or yellow; mild, medium, or sharp; young or aged

Cheshire

Colby

Comté

Crescenza

Double Gloucester

Edam

Fontina

Gouda, red wax, black wax, smoked, or aged; goat's or cow's milk

Gruyère

Havarti (including with dill, horse-radish, or other flavorings)

Ibérico

Jack, Monterey or Sonoma Jack (including with garlic, peppers, or herbs)

Jarlsberg

Mahón

Manchego

Mimolette

Mozzarella

Muenster

Ossau-Iraty

Port Salut

Provolone

P'tit Basque

Queso Oaxaca

Raclette

Roncal

Sage Derby

Scamorza (smoked mozzarella)

Swiss

Teleme

Toma

Urgelia

START WITH A PLAN

If you want to design your own grilled cheese masterpiece, which we highly recommend, you will need to put some thought into the combination of flavors you put together. When we are building a new sandwich, we have a few tried-and-true techniques for coming up with combinations that work. Even with tons of practice, we've found that it takes an average of three rounds of experiments to get it just right, so expect to make a few sandwiches and try a few different ingredients.

Plan A

Reimagine a favorite dish featuring cheese and turn it into a grilled cheese. We've turned pizzas (Hawaiian, margarita, pepperoni), pasta dishes (gnocchi Gorgonzola, butternut squash ravioli in brown butter and sage), and even salads (caprese, Greek) into grilled cheese sandwiches. You may need to tweak what goes where—for instance, we found we could get the sage flavor into the ravioli sandwich as a sage butter on the bread, and we roasted squash slices instead of using a purée, so the sandwich would have more texture and be less wet.

Plan B

Turn any sandwich into a grilled cheese. Many of our most popular grilled cheeses are variations on other sandwiches that aren't traditionally grilled cheeses. We've turned various regional specialties, like Reubens, Italian Beefs, Muffalettas, and tuna sandwiches into grilled cheeses. The trick with this plan is to remove things like lettuce that won't hold up well and to make the whole sandwich drier. Most grilled cheeses wouldn't be that awesome if they weren't cooked; they would taste dry. Typically, fresh lettuce, tomato, and mayo are added to sandwiches for moisture, but moisture is your enemy with a grilled cheese. Think about adding more cheese than the standard sandwich calls for (or adding cheese if it doesn't typically call for cheese) and removing ingredients that might make the sandwich soggy.

Plan C
Go regional. This strategy looks to traditional ingredients from a particular area and combines them in a grilled cheese. For instance, Morocco, New Mexico, California, and the Provence and Basque regions of France are all locations with unique herbs and spices, cheeses, breads, and other ingredients that we've explored. Pick your favorite regional cuisine and see if you can put traditional or unique flavors together in an interesting way.

COOKING TECHNIQUES: GO LOW AND SLOW
The term *grilled cheese* is actually a colloquialism for "griddled cheese"; we do not actually recommend grilling your cheese sandwich over an open flame on an outdoor grill. We use the traditional stove-top skillet method for the recipes in this book, but there are many other ways to cook a perfectly marvelous grilled cheese—almost as many ways as there are cheeses to try.

Following, we describe a variety of options you can use in addition to the pan-frying technique in most of our recipes, but the rule that applies to all is to keep it low and slow. Keep the temperature down and cook the sandwich slowly. This is especially important when you start adding in fillings like meats and vegetables that might take some time to heat through. In fact, the more stuff you put in your grilled cheese, the lower you want the heat, so that you can melt the cheese and warm the fillings while the bread toasts, without risk of burning.

Any of the following techniques work for the recipes in this book; we included some notes on which methods are better suited to which types of sandwiches.

Stove-Top Skillet
We use the stove-top skillet method for the recipes in this book because it is the method familiar to most folks, and also because it requires the least amount of special equipment: All you need is a burner, a large skillet, and a spatula . . . and the spatula is optional if you're reasonably dexterous with a fork or have well-callused fingertips. All burners are different. You'll need to do some experimentation to figure out what the optimal settings are for yours, so we recommend starting at medium-low heat and adjusting from there if you need to. Be aware that your skillet may get overly hot during preheating. You run the risk of burning your first sandwich if this happens. Generally it's better to put your sandwich in when the pan is too cool than when the pan is too hot—the worst that will happen if the pan is too cool is that your sandwich will take a little longer to cook. If your pan is smoking by the time you're ready to start cooking, cool it off by throwing in a

splash of cold water, then quickly swirling, and putting your sandwich in as soon as the water evaporates.

If you are cooking a grilled cheese with fillings, we recommend covering the pan with a lid. This holds in the heat and helps melt the cheese and warm the fillings faster and more evenly. The lid does not need to fit tightly; in fact, we often use a flat lid that is a little smaller than the pan, so the lid places just a little bit of weight on the sandwich while it cooks. This gentle pressure will help the bread make better contact with the pan surface and you'll get more even and thorough bread toasting as a result. If you are making a simple grilled cheese, or if you are cooking any of our breakfast grilled cheeses (which are cooked open-face before assembling), then the lid is unnecessary.

Advantages: All you need is a flat pan and a stove. It's easy to monitor and easy to clean up.

Disadvantages: Sandwiches with a lot of stuff in the middle can take a long time to cook, and the bread can get burnt before the cheese is melted. You can only cook one or two sandwiches at a time.

Electric or Gas Griddle

This method hardly needs an explanation, but there are a couple tricks to making reliably perfect grilled cheese on a gas griddle plate or electric griddle. Electric griddles are ideal: It's easy to control the heat, the sandwiches are unlikely to get burned, and the portable nature of the electric griddle means you can make grilled cheeses anywhere you can

run an extension cord. Heavy griddle plates designed to sit on top of stove-top burners also work very well, and just take a little more finesse to get and maintain the heat in the right zone. With either type of griddle, pre-heat to medium (about 350°F [180°C] for the electric griddle) and cook the sandwiches about 3 minutes per side. If the sandwiches have a lot of stuff in them, cover them with a heatproof cover or place a baking sheet on top while they're cooking to help retain the heat and put just a little pressure on the bread for even toasting.

Advantages: Electric griddles are extremely portable, so you can make grilled cheese at a party, the office, or anywhere you have access to power. Thicker griddles heat very evenly so sandwiches will cook up with a nice even crust. With the larger area, you can cook more sandwiches at the same time than a skillet on a stove top.

Disadvantages: If you don't own a griddle, you may not want to buy one just for this purpose. It can take some time for a thick griddle to heat up, and a thin griddle may cook unevenly.

Panini/Sandwich Press

Electric panini presses are, of course, engineered for making grilled cheese. You can use your panini press, pocket-style sandwich grill, or even a George Foreman Grill for all the sandwiches in this book except for the breakfast sandwiches. Because the panini press heats from both sides, the cooking time will be shorter and, of course, you do not need to flip the sandwich. Watch carefully and do not apply pressure to a grilled cheese in a panini press, or the hot cheese and fillings may smoosh out of the sandwich and create a stubborn mess on your press. There are many kinds of panini presses with different heat levels, so it may take some practice to figure out which setting on yours is ideal for the grilled cheeses in this book, but we recommend starting on the lower end of the thermostat, since many of our sandwiches have a lot of stuff in them to warm through without scorching the bread.

Advantages: A consistently crunchy crust that is unlikely to burn, thorough and consistent heating of fillings and melting of cheese, and very little cleanup. If you're cooking for one or two people, this is a great choice. You don't need any special equipment or utensils, aside, of course, from the panini press itself.

Disadvantages: You can only cook one or two sandwiches at a time, fillings may squish out, and the bread will be smooshed, which in our opinion is not the traditional grilled cheese profile.

The Oven Combo Method
The oven combo method is our go-to method when we are making grilled cheeses for four or more people. Using your oven and a skillet or griddle together, you can crank out four to twenty grilled cheeses in no time, which is why we specify this method for the Grilled Cheese Birthday Cake (page 90), which is a "cake" assembled out of twenty-four grilled cheeses.

To use this method, place a baking sheet or a large cast-iron skillet in your oven on the center rack and preheat to 350°F [180°C]. Assemble your grilled cheeses open-faced on a cutting board while the oven is heating. Place the cheese on top of each slice of bread and then the filling ingredients (if any) on top of the cheese, putting approximately equal amounts of ingredients on both halves of the sandwich. When your sandwiches are assembled and the oven is hot, transfer the open-faced sandwich halves to the hot baking sheet in the oven and cook for about 2 minutes (less if the sandwiches just have cheese, possibly more if they are sandwiches with a lot of stuff on them), or just until the cheese is beginning to look melted. The bread will likely not be toasted enough, so you'll need to finish the toasting in a skillet or on a griddle. While the sandwiches are in the oven, preheat an electric or gas griddle to medium, or place a cast-iron or nonstick skillet over medium-low heat. After removing the baking sheet with the sandwiches from the oven, close the sandwiches by placing one half on top of the other, filling-side down, and then place the assembled sandwiches on the hot griddle or in the hot skillet on the stove top to finish toasting; the sandwiches will toast quickly, in under 1 minute. Flip and toast the other side, cut in half, and serve immediately. If you are making a lot of sandwiches, say more than eight, this method works best with two people—one person manning the oven for melting and one person manning the griddle or skillet for toasting.

You can use this method with the break-fast sandwiches that feature eggs; just cook the eggs in a nonstick skillet while the sandwiches are in the oven melting, then replace the eggs with the open-faced sandwiches in the skillet, placing the cooked egg on top of the sandwich to rest while the bread toasts.

Advantages: The best choice for speed and volume, and all the cheeses and fillings will melt evenly.

Disadvantages: Difficult to get the timing right with a bunch of sandwiches going from oven to griddle, and a little tricky for one person to do alone; dirties several pans. It can be easy to overmelt sandwiches that just have cheese, like the Mousetrap Grilled Cheese (page 38) or Ultimate California Grilled Cheese (page 45); we recommend sticking to the stove-top method described in the recipes for these sandwiches.

DON'T TRY THESE AT HOME
Our insurance company says we can't actually recommend trying any of these techniques. In fact, they've asked us to actively discourage you from trying several of them. But we just have to share some of the more extreme ways we've cooked grilled cheeses.

Old-Fashioned Sandwich Iron
If you ever run across one of these, give it a try—they're so cool, and you can make an amazing grilled cheese while camping! Sandwich irons are antique tools used to cook a grilled cheese (or other hot sandwiches) over an open flame like a campfire or in a fireplace.

Place the sandwich inside the iron and close tightly, squishing the sandwich as much as needed to get a tight seal. Cook the sandwich in the iron over the open flame until toasty and hot. It can be a bit of a trick to figure out when the sandwich is done and which part of the fire is best for this technique, so be prepared for a bit of trial and error. Also, sandwich irons are usually pretty small (people had smaller appetites in those days), so don't get too ambitious with the fillings.

Waffle Iron
A waffle iron is basically a panini press with dents, right? The grilled cheeses without fillings, like the Mousetrap Grilled Cheese (page 38) and the Basque Sheep Grilled Cheese (page 40) will cook up nicely in a waffle iron. Sandwiches with a bunch of fillings, especially wet stuff like tomatoes, will just make a mess or not heat all the way through. This technique is not recommended unless you're really desperate for a grilled cheese, which, of course, is how we know about it.

Clothes Iron
Yep, in a pinch you can use a clothes iron to make grilled cheese. It won't make the best grilled cheese you've ever had, but it's a great way to impress children. Set the iron to medium heat and do not use steam. Also do not expect to be able to use your iron on your clothes after attempting this feat, unless you really want to smell like grilled cheese.

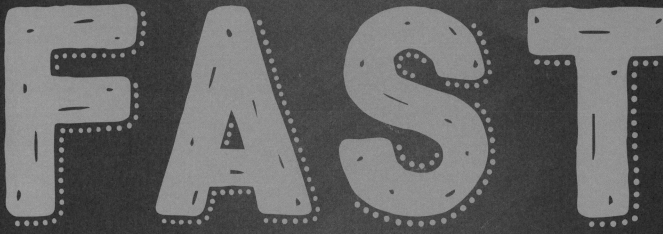

It's true! You can eat a grilled cheese for breakfast. Just by adding a fried egg, you can create fast, delicious, and filling breakfast sandwiches with every flavor profile you can imagine. The ideas for our popular breakfast grilled cheeses came from a couple of different directions. We found that we could add an egg in the middle of almost any sandwich on our lunch menu and magically it became "breakfast"; we also turned several traditional breakfast dishes into grilled cheeses. Huevos rancheros become Huevos Rollando Grilled Cheese (page 30). The old-fashioned Monte Cristo, a ham-and-cheese sandwich battered and fried and served with jam, has been modernized into the Sunday Brunch Grilled Cheese (page 32), a collection of savory-sweet grilled cheeses using eggy challah or brioche breads, which are battered and griddled and then stuffed with a variety of fruits and cheeses.

If you are concerned about eating undercooked eggs, many groceries carry pasteurized whole eggs in the shell, or go ahead and burst the yolk with a fork before you flip it, and you'll have a fried egg over-hard. A scrambled egg is also delicious in these sandwiches; just leave the scrambled egg a little soft, as it will keep cooking even after it is out of the pan.

CLASSIC BREAKFAST
GRILLED CHEESE

SERVES 1

Want to up the ante (and the protein) on any grilled cheese? Add an egg. This is a fast and hearty breakfast sandwich that will definitely keep you satiated until lunch. If you assemble the uncooked sandwich—without the egg—the evening before, then wrap it in plastic and refrigerate, you can make this in minutes in the morning and be out the door with a warm, gooey breakfast in hand. Just bring an extra napkin—especially if you like your eggs over easy, like we do.

1½ tsp salted butter, at room temperature

2 slices rustic artisan whole-wheat or whole-grain bread

1 slice medium or sharp Cheddar cheese

1 slice Monterey Jack or Sonoma Jack cheese

1 egg

Kosher salt and freshly ground black pepper

1) Heat a nonstick skillet over medium-low heat.

2) Spread the butter on one side of each bread slice, dividing it evenly. Place both slices, buttered-side down, on a clean cutting board. Place the Cheddar on one slice of bread and the Jack on the other.

3) Using a wide spatula, transfer the breads, buttered-side down, to the hot skillet. Coat a clear area in the pan with nonstick cooking spray, then carefully crack the egg into the greased space. Sprinkle the egg with salt and pepper.

4) While the egg is cooking, keep an eye on your breads. When the bottoms are nicely browned and the cheese is melted, about 2 minutes, return them to the cutting board. When the egg white is mostly cooked through, carefully flip the egg with a silicone spatula. (Don't worry if you break the yolk; it will still be delicious.) Cook for about 30 seconds longer, or until the egg white is fully cooked but the yolk is still soft.

5) Slide the fried egg on top of the melted cheese on one bread slice and gently place the other bread on top, cheese-side down. Cut the sandwich in half, if desired, and serve immediately.

BREAKFAST-IN-BED
GRILLED CHEESE

SERVES 1

Who doesn't love breakfast in bed? Especially when it involves a gooey, decadent grilled cheese. We developed this sandwich after trying an amazing fenugreek Gouda at a cheese tasting event; fenugreek, a fragrant and soothing spice often used in curries, smells just like maple syrup when toasted. We went with the brunch theme and paired the fenugreek Gouda with Barely Buzzed, a unique Cheddar made by the Beehive Cheese Co. of Utah that is rubbed with coffee and lavender, and added an egg and bacon—all conjuring a dreamy and delicious start to the day.

The recommended way to eat this sandwich is in your pajamas on a Saturday morning, while watching cartoons. This isn't a regular item on the menu at our restaurant, but we serve it at special events and it's always a hit.

1½ tsp salted butter, at room temperature

2 slices rustic artisan bread such as levain, sourdough, or white

1 slice fenugreek Gouda cheese

1 slice Barely Buzzed Cheddar cheese (see Sources, page 168)

1 egg

Kosher salt and freshly ground black pepper

2 strips thick-sliced bacon, cooked until crisp and drained

1) Heat a nonstick skillet over medium-low heat.

2) Spread the butter on one side of each bread slice, dividing it evenly. Place both slices, buttered-side down, on a clean cutting board. Place the Gouda on one slice of bread and the Cheddar on the other.

3) Using a wide spatula, transfer the breads, buttered-side down, to the hot skillet. Coat a clear area in the pan with nonstick cooking spray, then carefully crack the egg into the greased space. Sprinkle the egg with salt and pepper.

4) While the egg is cooking, keep an eye on your breads. When the bottoms are nicely browned and the cheese is melted, about 2 minutes, return them to the cutting board. When the egg white is mostly cooked through, carefully flip the egg with a silicone spatula. (Don't worry if you break the yolk; it will still be delicious.) Cook for about 30 seconds longer, or until the egg white is fully cooked but the yolk is still soft.

5) Arrange the bacon strips on top of the melted cheese on one bread slice, slide the fried egg onto the bacon, and gently place the other bread on top, cheese-side down. Cut the sandwich in half, if desired, and serve immediately.

BREAKFAST POPPER
GRILLED CHEESE

SERVES 1

There's some kind of alchemy that happens when you mix fats—cheese and egg yolks—with hot chiles. The chiles are tamed, the fat is cut, and everything is made more delicious.

The Jalapeño Popper Grilled Cheese (page 68) was already on the menu and a staff favorite when a great idea was hatched. A couple of our cooks started adding eggs to the lunch sandwich and eating it for breakfast. Egged on, soon the Breakfast Popper became the de facto staff eye-opener of choice. Eventually we realized customers would like it, too, and put it on the menu, where it has attained a cult following.

1½ tsp salted butter, at room temperature

2 slices rustic artisan bread such as levain, sourdough, or white

1 Tbsp chèvre (goat cheese), at room temperature

¼ cup [55 g] Apricot-Jalapeño Relish (page 155)

1 slice Monterey Jack or Sonoma Jack cheese

1 egg

Kosher salt and freshly ground black pepper

2 strips thick-sliced bacon, cooked until crisp and drained

1) Heat a nonstick skillet over medium-low heat.

2) Spread the butter on one side of each bread slice, dividing it evenly. Place both slices, buttered-side down, on a clean cutting board. Spread the chèvre on one slice of bread and the relish on the other. Place the Jack on top of the relish.

3) Using a wide spatula, transfer the breads, buttered-side down, to the hot skillet. Coat a clear area in the pan with nonstick cooking spray, then carefully crack the egg into the greased space. Sprinkle the egg with salt and pepper.

4) While the egg is cooking, keep an eye on your breads. When the bottoms are nicely browned and the cheese is melted, about 2 minutes, return them to the cutting board. When the egg white is mostly cooked through, carefully flip the egg with a silicone spatula. (Don't worry if you break the yolk; it will still be delicious.) Cook for about 30 seconds longer, or until the egg white is fully cooked but the yolk is still soft.

5) Arrange the bacon strips on top of the melted Jack, slide the fried egg onto the bacon, and gently place the other bread on top, cheese-side down. Cut the sandwich in half, if desired, and serve immediately.

FARMER'S BREAKFAST
GRILLED CHEESE

SERVES 2

A hearty greeting for waker-uppers in any field, the much-beloved classic combo of home fries, bacon, eggs, and toast with butter transforms beautifully into a perfect breakfast sandwich. A pinch of pungent fresh chives pairs so well with these flavors, I couldn't resist adding them to the grilling butter—they also contribute a touch of bright green to balance the warm palette of Cheddar and roasted potatoes.

I know, potatoes in a grilled cheese sandwich may seem a little weird. But trust me, the textures work together wonderfully, and the sturdy potato slices add a nice structure to the sandwich and help hold everything together.

1 small waxy-skinned potato such as Yukon gold, scrubbed and cut into ¼-in [6-mm] rounds

1 tsp olive oil

Kosher salt and freshly ground black pepper

1 Tbsp salted butter, at room temperature

4 fresh chives, minced or snipped

4 slices rustic artisan bread such as levain, sourdough, or white

4 slices medium or sharp Cheddar cheese

2 eggs

4 strips thick-sliced bacon, cooked until crisp and drained

1) Heat the oven to 425°F [220°C]. Coat a baking sheet with nonstick cooking spray or line it with parchment paper.

2) In a bowl, combine the potato slices with the olive oil and a pinch each of salt and pepper and toss gently until the potatoes are evenly coated. Spread the potatoes in a single layer on the prepared baking sheet. Roast until cooked through and starting to brown in spots, about 15 minutes. Set aside to cool. (Store, covered, in the refrigerator for up to 2 days. Reheat for about 20 seconds in a microwave oven before using.)

3) Heat a nonstick skillet over medium-low heat.

4) In a small bowl, stir together the butter and chives until well blended.

5) Spread half the chive butter on one side of two of the bread slices, dividing it evenly. Place both slices, buttered-side down, on a clean cutting board. Place one slice of Cheddar on each bread slice and then place three or four warm potato slices on top of the cheese on one slice of bread.

6) Using a wide spatula, transfer the two breads, buttered-side down, to the hot skillet. Coat a clear area in the pan with nonstick cooking spray, then carefully crack one of the eggs into the greased space. Sprinkle the egg with salt and pepper.

7) While the egg is cooking, keep an eye on your breads. When the bottoms are nicely browned and the cheese is melted, about 2 minutes, return them to the cutting board. When the egg white is mostly cooked through, carefully flip the egg with a silicone spatula. (Don't worry if you break the yolk; it will still be delicious.) Cook for about 30 seconds longer, or until the egg white is fully cooked but the yolk is still soft.

8) Arrange two of the bacon strips on top of the potatoes, slide the fried egg onto the bacon, and gently place the other bread on top, cheese-side down. Cut the sandwich in half, if desired, and serve. Repeat to cook and assemble the second sandwich. (Save any leftover potatoes for another use.)

BREAKFAST PIGLET
GRILLED CHEESE

SERVES 2

Our popular breakfast sandwiches all started with the Breakfast Piglet Grilled Cheese: One hungry morning I had the idea of adding an egg to the Piglet Grilled Cheese (page 69) for my own breakfast, and *ta-da*—warm, melty magic. Apples, ham, and rosemary are already best friends with sharp Cheddar cheese, and the rich egg just puts the whole sandwich over the top. One of our favorite customers likes his with oven-roasted tomatoes, and that became our second-favorite addition to this sandwich—tomato lovers, give it a try!

1 Tbsp salted butter, at room temperature

1 tsp minced fresh rosemary or ½ tsp dried rosemary, crumbled

4 slices rustic artisan bread such as levain, sourdough, or white

2 Tbsp Apple Mustard (page 160)

4 slices mild, medium, or sharp Cheddar cheese

4 oz [115 g] thinly sliced ham

2 eggs

Kosher salt and freshly ground black pepper

1) Heat a nonstick skillet over medium-low heat.

2) In a small bowl, stir together the butter and rosemary until well blended.

3) Spread half the rosemary butter on one side of two of the bread slices, dividing it evenly. Place both slices, buttered-side down, on a clean cutting board. Spread 1 Tbsp of the apple mustard on one slice of bread. Layer one slice of the Cheddar and half of the ham on top of the mustard. Arrange another slice of the Cheddar on the other piece of bread.

4) Using a wide spatula, transfer the two breads, buttered-side down, to the hot skillet. Coat a clear area in the pan with nonstick cooking spray, then carefully crack one of the eggs into the greased space. Sprinkle the egg with salt and pepper.

5) While the egg is cooking, keep an eye on your breads. When the bottoms are nicely browned and the cheese is melted, about 2 minutes, return them to the cutting board. When the egg white is mostly cooked through, carefully flip the egg with a silicone spatula. (Don't worry if you break the yolk; it will still be delicious.) Cook for about 30 seconds longer, or until the egg white is fully cooked but the yolk is still soft.

6) Slide the fried egg on top of the ham and gently place the other bread on top, cheese-side down. Cut the sandwich in half, if desired, and serve. Repeat to cook and assemble the second sandwich.

GREEN EGGS AND HAM
GRILLED CHEESE

SERVES 2

Well, technically (and happily) the eggs aren't green—the beautiful marbled hue of sage-flavored Derby cheese supplies the color, and in a very tasty way. I came up with this special to celebrate Dr. Seuss Day (March 2). The whole staff at the restaurant came to work in pajamas, and I made the mistake of wearing a footie onesie, which was a problem on two fronts: It got astonishingly hot in the flannel fabric, and the feet were not exactly slip-proof—I slid around the kitchen all day. I resolved that next time I would wear my favorite Wonder Woman pajamas; they have much better air flow.

1 Tbsp salted butter, at room temperature

1 tsp minced fresh sage or ½ tsp dried rubbed sage

4 slices challah or *pain de mie*

4 slices sage Derby cheese

4 oz [115 g] thinly sliced ham

2 eggs

Kosher salt and freshly ground black pepper

1) Heat a nonstick skillet over medium-low heat.

2) In a small bowl, stir together the butter and sage until well blended.

3) Spread half the sage butter on one side of two of the bread slices, dividing it evenly. Place both slices, buttered-side down, on a clean cutting board. Place one slice of the Derby on each bread slice, then lay half of the ham on top of the cheese on one slice.

4) Using a wide spatula, transfer the two breads, buttered-side down, to the hot skillet. Coat a clear area in the pan with nonstick cooking spray, then carefully crack one of the eggs into the greased space. Sprinkle the egg with salt and pepper.

5) While the egg is cooking, keep an eye on your breads. When the bottoms are nicely browned and the cheese is melted, about 2 minutes, return them to the cutting board. When the egg white is mostly cooked through, carefully flip the egg with a silicone spatula. (Don't worry if you break the yolk; it will still be delicious.) Cook for about 30 seconds longer, or until the egg white is fully cooked but the yolk is still soft.

6) Slide the fried egg on top of the ham and gently place the other bread on top, cheese-side down. Cut the sandwich in half, if desired, and serve. Repeat to cook and assemble the second sandwich.

HUEVOS ROLLANDO
GRILLED CHEESE

SERVES 4

Huevos rancheros in the form of a grilled cheese? *Bueno!* Rollando is the middle name of one of the cooks who helped us develop this sandwich, so we named it after him. It's a great savory brunch option, or try breakfast for dinner and serve it in the evening. Adjust the level of spicy heat to your own taste by using mild—or thermonuclear—hot sauce. You'll want to serve this sandwich with a knife and fork—it gets messy!

BLACK BEAN RANCHERO MIX

1 tsp olive oil

½ small yellow onion, finely chopped

1 garlic clove, minced

1 tsp ground cumin

½ tsp kosher salt

½ tsp freshly ground black pepper

One 15-oz [425-g] can black beans, drained and rinsed

One 7-oz [198-g] can ranchero sauce *(salsa ranchera)*

½ tsp hot sauce, or more to taste

2 Tbsp salted butter, at room temperature

½ tsp chipotle chile powder

8 slices rustic artisan bread such as levain, sourdough, or white

8 slices pepper Jack or habanero Jack cheese

1 small ripe plum tomato, cut into ¼-in [6-mm] dice

4 eggs

Kosher salt and freshly ground black pepper

1 ripe avocado, preferably Hass, pitted, peeled, and cut into slices about ¼ in [6 mm] thick

Sour cream for topping

Pico de gallo **or other salsa of your choice for serving**

1) To make the black bean ranchero mix: In a small saucepan over medium heat, warm the olive oil. Add the onion and sauté until translucent, 5 to 7 minutes. Stir in the garlic, cumin, salt, and pepper and sauté for 1 minute longer. Stir in the beans, ranchero sauce, and hot sauce and turn the heat to low. Simmer until the mixture is thickened, about 10 minutes, stirring occasionally. Cover to keep warm and set aside. (Store, covered, in the refrigerator for up to 2 days. Reheat for about 20 seconds in a microwave oven before using.)

2) Heat a nonstick skillet over medium-low heat.

3) In a small bowl, stir together the butter and chipotle chile powder until well blended.

4) Spread the chipotle butter on one side of each bread slice, dividing it evenly. Place two of the slices, buttered-side down, on a clean cutting board. Place one slice of the pepper Jack on each. Spoon about ¼ cup [75 g] of the ranchero bean mix on top of the Jack on one slice and sprinkle one-fourth of the diced tomato on top of the beans.

5) Using a wide spatula, transfer the two breads, buttered-side down, to the hot skillet. Coat a clear area in the pan with nonstick cooking spray, then carefully crack one of the eggs into the greased space. Sprinkle the egg with salt and pepper.

6) While the egg is cooking, keep an eye on your breads. When the bottoms are nicely browned and the cheese is melted, about 2 minutes, return them to the cutting board. When the egg white is mostly cooked through, carefully flip the egg with a silicone spatula. (Don't worry if you break the yolk; it will still be delicious.) Cook for about 30 seconds longer, or until the egg white is fully cooked but the yolk is still soft.

7) Slide the fried egg on top of the tomato, top with one-fourth of the avocado slices, and gently place the other bread on top, cheese-side down. Cut the sandwich in half, if desired, and top with a dollop of sour cream. Repeat to cook and assemble the remaining sandwiches. Serve, passing the *pico de gallo* at the table.

SUNDAY BRUNCH
GRILLED CHEESE

SERVES 4

Inspired by the magnificent Monte Cristo—a ham-and-cheese sandwich that is battered and fried and then dusted with powdered sugar and served with maple syrup or jam—I experimented with different breads, flavorings, fruits, cheeses, and garnishes to make a French toast–style sandwich that is uniquely ours. For the essential bread itself, I found that marrying slightly dry slices of brioche loaf with a thick batter enriched with butter, vanilla, and flour yields both a nice, crisp and dry finish on the outside of the cooked sandwich and a perfect custardy consistency on the inside.

Following are three of our favorite variations for this fabulous assembly—merely a hint at the wide range of different sweet and savory fillings that can make for a very sophisticated brunch sandwich.

One 1-lb [455-g] brioche or challah loaf, cut into 8 thick slices

¾ cup [180 ml] whole milk

1 egg, lightly beaten

4 Tbsp salted butter; 2 Tbsp melted, 2 Tbsp at room temperature

2 tsp vanilla extract

2 tsp granulated sugar

½ cup [60 g] all-purpose flour

¼ tsp kosher salt

4 oz [115 g] Brie or triple crème cheese, thinly sliced

8 ripe strawberries, hulled and thinly sliced

Confectioners' sugar for dusting

Brown Sugar Bourbon Sauce (page 35) for drizzling

1) Arrange the bread slices on a large baking sheet and let dry while preparing the other ingredients.

2) In a medium bowl, whisk together the milk, egg, melted butter, and vanilla. Add the granulated sugar, flour, and salt and whisk to combine. Scrape the batter into a shallow pan, such as a pie dish or cake pan. Set aside.

3) Heat a stove-top griddle pan or a large cast-iron skillet over medium-low heat, or heat an electric griddle to 350°F [180°C].

4) When the griddle is hot, nestle two slices of the bread in the batter and let soak for 5 seconds, then carefully flip and soak on the second side for another 5 seconds. Transfer the soaked breads to a clean plate. Melt ½ Tbsp of the room-temperature butter on the hot griddle and add both pieces of the soaked bread. Cook until the first sides are nicely browned and completely dry to the touch, about 3 minutes. Using a wide spatula, carefully turn the breads.

CONT'D

5) While the second sides are cooking, arrange one-fourth of the Brie and one-fourth of the strawberries on top of one piece of bread. When the second sides are nicely browned and the Brie is just softened, use the spatula to transfer the bread with the cheese and strawberries to a platter and gently place the other cooked bread on top. Cover loosely with aluminum foil and place in a low oven to keep warm. Repeat to cook and assemble the remaining sandwiches.

6) Place each sandwich on a plate; cut in half, if desired; dust with confectioners' sugar; drizzle with the bourbon sauce; and serve immediately.

Variations

Chèvre and Fig Chutney: Substitute 6 Tbsp [85 g] room-temperature chèvre (goat cheese) for the Brie and ½ cup [110 g] fig chutney for the strawberries.

Cristo Hispanico: Substitute 3 oz [85 g] thinly sliced Manchego cheese for the Brie and pile 3 oz [85 g] shaved or thinly sliced *Jamón Serrano,* prosciutto, or speck on top; substitute ¼ cup [55 g] pumpkin-orange marmalade for the strawberries. Garnish with fresh raspberries.

Honey Pot: Substitute ¼ cup [55 g] room-temperature chèvre and 3 oz [85 g] shaved or thinly sliced Carmody cheese for the Brie and top with 3 oz [85 g] thinly sliced French-style ham. Substitute ¼ cup [55 g] tomato jam for the strawberries. There is no honey in this sandwich; the name "Honey Pot" refers to the category in a grilled cheese competition that this sandwich won.

BROWN SUGAR-BOURBON SAUCE

MAKES ABOUT 1½ CUPS [360 ML]

We use this incredibly easy and delicious dessert sauce on our bread pudding and Sunday Brunch Grilled Cheese sandwiches. Drizzle it over ice cream, cheesecake, pancakes, or waffles for a sophisticated treat.

Make this sauce your own! Instead of bourbon, feel free to substitute rum, rye, amaretto, orange brandy, or applejack (apple brandy) for different flavors.

1 cup [200 g] packed dark brown sugar

1/2 cup [110 g] salted butter, at room temperature

1/2 cup [120 ml] heavy cream

2 Tbsp bourbon

2 tsp vanilla extract

1) In a small saucepan over medium-low heat, melt the brown sugar and butter together, whisking constantly until smooth.

2) Turn the heat to low and carefully add the cream, bourbon, and vanilla (the mixture may boil up at this point, so add the liquids slowly and keep whisking constantly). Bring the sauce to a simmer and cook for 5 minutes, whisking occasionally, or until slightly thickened. Remove from the heat and let the sauce cool for 5 to 10 minutes before using.

3) Store in an airtight container in the refrigerator for up to 1 month. Reheat in a microwave when you're ready to serve.

GRILLED CHEESE SANDWICHES

You could say our tastes became more sophisticated as Nate and I grew up, in our own kitchen and as chefs and restaurateurs, but we never outgrew our love of grilled cheese. In this chapter, we have included our favorite grilled cheese recipes, ranging from the simple and traditional Mousetrap Grilled Cheese (page 38) to grown-up variations like the Moroccan Chicken Grilled Cheese (page 58) topped with exotic spices and a spread of Castelvetrano olives and preserved Meyer lemons. There are grilled cheeses you can make in a few minutes using ingredients from a decent corner store, and also more adventurous options that take some preparation and specialty foods shopping but will reward you with a unique grilled cheese experience.

Grilled cheese is a forgiving dish. We encourage you to make substitutions and customizations, based on what ingredients are available to you and also your own tastes. If a particular bread or cheese that we specify can't be found, look for something similar and you'll likely get great results. Quantities of ingredients can also be adjusted; if the loaf of bread you're using yields slices that are larger or smaller than average, you may need more or less cheese, butter, or fillings.

MOUSETRAP
GRILLED CHEESE

SERVES 1

The Mousetrap Grilled Cheese is deceptively simple—bread, butter, cheese—but we spent more time developing this sandwich than any other. When we started working on this dish, the goal was to differentiate our definitive grilled cheese from every other rendition out there, including your grandma's. It had to be nostalgic, familiar, perfectly gooey, and perfectly toasted, and not greasy but with a distinct buttery-ness.

We decided to build a better mousetrap—hence the name. We tested a dozen breads, two dozen cheeses, and three kinds of butter. We experimented with mayonnaise (which will work in place of the butter, if that's all you have), buttering the inside of the bread, cooking the sandwich open-faced, shredding the cheese, slicing the cheese—every iteration you can imagine—until we felt we had created the perfect monument to bread, cheese, and Grandma. Now we serve more Mousetraps than anything else on the menu. Snap.

1) Heat a cast-iron or nonstick skillet over medium-low heat.

2) Spread the butter on one side of each bread slice, dividing it evenly. Place one slice, buttered-side down, on a clean cutting board. Layer the Cheddar, Havarti, and Jack on top. Finish with the second slice of bread, buttered-side up.

3) Using a wide spatula, place the sandwich in the pan, cover, and cook until the bottom is nicely browned, 2 to 3 minutes. Turn and cook until the second side is browned and the cheese is melted, about 2 minutes longer.

4) Cut the sandwich in half, if desired, and serve immediately.

1½ tsp salted butter, at room temperature

2 slices California sourdough bread

1 slice medium Cheddar cheese

1 slice Havarti cheese

1 slice Monterey Jack cheese

MAKE IT YOUR OWN

At the restaurant, we offer a variety of substitutions and add-ons, and many of our regular customers have their own favorite combinations for the Mousetrap as well as other customizations of sandwiches. I encourage you to experiment with different breads, cheeses, and add-ons. Below is a list of suggestions to get you started.

Breads: *Pain de mie,* whole wheat, multigrain, high-quality white, rustic sourdough, or levain.

Cheeses: Mild or sharp Cheddars, garlic or pepper Jack, dill- or other flavored Havarti, mild fontina, Comté, Gouda. A combination of semihard and semisoft cheeses is ideal.

Fillings: Add any of these fillings between the Cheddar and Havarti—sautéed arugula or spinach; sliced fresh or oven-roasted tomatoes; tomato or onion jam; cooked bacon; sliced ham; sliced roast beef; sliced roast chicken; mustard; bread 'n' butter pickles; roasted bell peppers; fresh, pickled, or canned diced jalapeños; grilled or caramelized onions; thinly sliced green apples.

BASQUE SHEEP
GRILLED CHEESE

SERVES 1

P'tit Basque is a sheep's-milk cheese made in France's Pyrenees Mountains. It's sweet and creamy with nutty flavors, and melts beautifully. Ossau-Iraty, another semihard sheep's-milk cheese from the Basque region, is a substitution *très bon*. With a pinch of herbes de Provence mixed into the butter, eating this sandwich is like going on a quick trip to France. Enjoy with a chilled glass of French rosé. You can use store-bought herbes de Provence if you wish, but it's surprisingly easy to make your own, and this versatile spice mix can be used to dress up many other dishes.

1½ tsp salted butter, at room temperature

¼ tsp Herbes de Provence (facing page)

1 tsp wildflower honey

1 tsp Dijon mustard

2 slices French bread

2 oz [55 g] P'tit Basque or Ossau-Iraty cheese, sliced

1) Heat a cast-iron or nonstick skillet over medium-low heat.

2) In a small bowl, stir together the butter and herbes de Provence until well blended. In another small bowl, stir together the honey and mustard.

3) Spread the herbes de Provence butter on one side of each bread slice, dividing it evenly. Place both slices, buttered-side down, on a clean cutting board. Spread the honey mustard on one slice. Place the P'tit Basque on top. Finish with the second slice of bread, buttered-side up.

4) Using a wide spatula, place the sandwich in the pan, cover, and cook until the bottom is nicely browned, 2 to 3 minutes. Turn and cook until the second side is browned and the cheese is melted, about 2 minutes longer.

5) Cut the sandwich in half, if desired, and serve immediately.

HERBES DE PROVENCE

MAKES ABOUT ¼ CUP [15 G]

Herbes de Provence is a blend of herbs that grow (as you may have guessed) in Provence. The components and formulation vary, but thyme, savory, and lavender are almost always included, and these fresh herbal flavors are interesting, refreshing, and satisfying in a grilled cheese. You can also use herbes de Provence on grilled fish or meats, in vegetable stews, or in salad dressings, among many uses.

2 tsp dried thyme

2 tsp dried rosemary

2 tsp dried lavender buds

1 tsp fennel seeds

2 tsp dried oregano

2 tsp dried savory

2 tsp dried marjoram

1 tsp dried basil

1) Combine the thyme, rosemary, lavender buds, and fennel seeds in a mortar and grind to a coarse powder using a pestle, or grind in a spice grinder or a coffee grinder dedicated to spices. (We use a dedicated coffee grinder for this purpose, but you can use your regular coffee grinder and just wipe it out carefully before and after grinding the herbs.)

2) In a small bowl, stir together the ground herbs, oregano, savory, marjoram, and basil until thoroughly blended.

3) Store in an airtight container in a cool, dark place for up to 3 months.

MAC 'N' CHEESE
GRILLED CHEESE

SERVES 8

This sandwich has blown many a ten-year-old's mind. "Mac 'n' cheese . . . in a grilled cheese!?!" It sounds a little crazy, but it's a lot delicious. Because the rich mac filling is chilled in a thin layer on a baking sheet, the recipe isn't easily scaled down to one or two servings; but you don't need to use all the mac at once. Well-wrapped, it will keep for up to 3 days in the refrigerator or up to 1 month in the freezer, so portion it individually and blow minds at your own pace.

MAC 'N' CHEESE

8 oz [230 g] elbow, spiral, or other short pasta of your choice

⅓ cup [40 g] all-purpose flour

¾ tsp dry mustard powder

½ tsp garlic powder

½ tsp kosher salt

½ tsp freshly ground black pepper

⅛ tsp cayenne pepper

6 Tbsp [85 g] salted butter, at room temperature

1½ cups [360 ml] whole milk

1 cup [240 ml] heavy cream

1 lb [455 g] cheese (any combination of Monterey Jack, Cheddar, Colby, fontina, or Gouda), shredded

4 Tbsp [55 g] salted butter, at room temperature

1 tsp garlic powder

16 slices square sourdough, whole-wheat, or other sandwich loaf bread

8 slices mild, medium, or sharp Cheddar cheese

8 slices Monterey Jack or Colby Jack cheese

1) To make the mac 'n' cheese: Bring a medium saucepan of generously salted water (so it tastes like seawater) to a boil over high heat. Add the pasta and stir immediately. Boil the pasta, stirring occasionally, just until al dente, 8 to 10 minutes or according to the package directions (the pasta should be tender but still chewy, not mushy). Drain the pasta in a colander and set aside.

2) While the pasta is cooking, in a small bowl, whisk together the flour, mustard powder, garlic powder, salt, black pepper, and cayenne pepper and set aside.

3) Put the empty pasta pan (no need to wash it) over low heat and add the butter. When the butter is melted, whisk in the flour mixture. Cook, whisking often, until the mixture is beginning to brown and has a pleasant, nutty aroma, about 1 minute. Watch carefully so it does not burn.

CONT'D

4) Slowly whisk the milk and cream into the butter-flour mixture, combining well. Cook, whisking constantly, until the sauce is heated through and just begins to thicken, about 2 minutes. Remove from the heat. Add the cheese gradually while stirring constantly in one direction with a wooden spoon or silicone spatula. Stir until the cheese has melted into the sauce, then stir in the cooked pasta.

5) Line a 9-by-13-in [23-by-33-cm] rimmed baking sheet with parchment paper (or aluminum foil, in a pinch). Coat the parchment paper with nonstick cooking spray, then pour the warm mac 'n' cheese into the prepared baking sheet and spread evenly with a spatula. Coat another piece of parchment paper with cooking spray and place, oiled-side down, directly on the surface of the mac 'n' cheese. Refrigerate until cool and firm, about 1 hour.

6) Heat a large cast-iron or nonstick skillet over medium-low heat.

7) In a small bowl, stir together the 4 Tbsp [55 g] butter and garlic powder until well blended. Set aside.

8) Remove the mac 'n' cheese from the refrigerator and peel off the top layer of parchment paper. Carefully cut into eight equal pieces.

9) Spread ¾ tsp of the garlic butter on one side of each bread slice. Place half of the slices, buttered-side down, on a clean cutting board. Top each with one slice of Cheddar, then one piece of the mac 'n' cheese. (Transfer from the baking sheet by scooting your hand or a spatula under each piece of mac 'n' cheese and then flipping it over onto a sandwich.) Place one slice of Jack on top of each. Finish with the remaining bread slices, buttered-side up.

10) Using a wide spatula, place as many sandwiches in the pan as will fit without crowding, cover, and cook until the bottoms are nicely browned, about 4 minutes. Turn and cook until the second sides are browned, the cheese is melted, and the mac 'n' cheese is heated through, about 4 minutes longer.

11) Cut the sandwiches in half, if desired, and serve. Repeat to cook the remaining sandwiches.

Variations

Crab Mac Grilled Cheese: Toss 8 oz [230 g] cooked lump crabmeat (fresh or canned, picked over for shell fragments and cartilage) with 2 Tbsp minced fresh flat-leaf parsley and 1 tsp lemon zest in a small bowl. When assembling the sandwiches, divide the crab mixture evenly on top of the mac filling before topping with the Jack and the second slice of bread.

Chili Mac Grilled Cheese: Add a big dollop of chili (see page 116) to the top of the mac 'n' cheese before topping with the Jack and the second slice of bread.

Tomato-Bacon-Jalapeño Mac Grilled Cheese: Layer 1 or 2 slices of fresh, ripe heirloom tomato, 2 slices of cooked, crisp bacon, and 2 tsp diced fresh jalapeños on top of the mac 'n' cheese before topping with the Jack and the second slice of bread.

ULTIMATE CALIFORNIA
GRILLED CHEESE

SERVES 1

San Francisco sourdough gets its distinctive tangy flavor from the wild yeasts native to the area, and you can't make it anywhere else in the world. Local bakers treat their sourdough starter like a child, watching it carefully and nurturing it just so, and each bakery's version is slightly different. If you can get your hands on a fresh loaf of sourdough and the handcrafted California cheeses we've listed in the recipe ingredients (see Sources, page 168), you'll have a very special sandwich. Substitute other high-quality semi-hard American cheeses, such as bandage-wrapped Cheddar, aged Jack, or Italian-style fontina if you can't find these, but stick as closely to this list as possible to experience a stunning and authentically Californian grilled cheese.

2 slices California sourdough

1½ tsp Napa Valley extra-virgin olive oil

1 slice Fiscalini San Joaquin Gold cheese

¼ ripe California Hass avocado, cut into slices about ¼ in [6 mm] thick (optional)

1 slice Bellwether Farms Carmody cheese

1 slice Point Reyes Farmstead Toma cheese

1) Heat a cast-iron or nonstick skillet over medium-low heat.

2) Brush one side of each bread slice with the olive oil. Place one slice, oiled-side down, on a clean cutting board. Layer the San Joaquin Gold, avocado (if using), Carmody, and Toma on top. Finish with the second slice of bread, oiled-side up.

3) Using a wide spatula, place the sandwich in the pan, cover, and cook until the bottom is nicely browned, 2 to 3 minutes. Turn and cook until the second side is browned and the cheese is melted, about 2 minutes longer.

4) Cut the sandwich in half, if desired, and serve immediately.

MUSHROOM-GRUYÈRE
GRILLED CHEESE

SERVES 2

Vegetarians love this sandwich, piled with a rich mix of earthy, tender mushrooms. The inspiration was an amazing fresh mushroom ravioli dish Nate and I had on vacation in Italy, perfumed with the aromas of thyme and other herbs and oozing delicious drips of fresh cream and Fontina Val d'Aosta, a creamy (and fairly stinky) aged cow's-milk cheese made in the tiny French-speaking Aosta Valley of Italy. Sautéed leeks put the dish over the top. If you are lucky enough to find Fontina Val d'Aosta in your local specialty cheese shop, pile it into this seriously decadent sandwich, *subito*!

1 Tbsp salted butter, at room temperature

1 tsp minced fresh thyme or ½ tsp dried thyme

1 small Yukon gold potato, peeled and cut into slices about ¼ in [6 mm] thick

2½ tsp olive oil

Kosher salt and freshly ground black pepper

1 small leek, trimmed and tough green tops removed, halved lengthwise and carefully washed, cut into ¼-in [6-mm] dice

2 oz [55 g] shiitake mushrooms, stemmed, brushed clean, and cut into slices about ⅛ in [3 mm] thick

2 oz [55 g] cremini mushrooms, brushed clean and cut into slices about ⅛ in [3 mm] thick

2 oz [55 g] oyster mushrooms, brushed clean and coarsely chopped

4 slices rustic artisan bread such as levain, sourdough, or white

2 thick slices Italian-style fontina cheese, preferably Fontina Val d'Aosta

2 thin slices Gruyère cheese

1) Preheat the oven to 425°F [220°C]. Line a baking sheet with parchment paper or coat thoroughly with nonstick cooking spray.

2) In a small bowl, stir together the butter and half of the thyme and set aside.

3) In a medium bowl, toss the potatoes with ½ tsp of the olive oil and a pinch each of salt and pepper until the potatoes are evenly coated. Spread the potatoes in a single layer on the prepared baking sheet and roast until cooked through and starting to brown in spots, about 15 minutes. Set aside to cool.

4) In a small saucepan over medium-low heat, warm 1 tsp of the olive oil. Add the leek and a pinch of salt and stir well. Cover and cook, stirring often to prevent sticking, until the leek is very soft, about 10 minutes. Remove from the heat and set aside.

5) In a medium sauté pan over medium-high heat, warm the remaining 1 tsp olive oil. Add all of the mushrooms, the remaining thyme, and a pinch each of salt and pepper. Sauté until the mushrooms have released their juices, are tender, and are just beginning to brown, 3 to 5 minutes. Set aside.

6) Heat a cast-iron or nonstick skillet over low heat.

7) Spread the thyme butter on one side of each bread slice, dividing it evenly. Place two slices, buttered-side down, on a clean cutting board. Spread about 1 Tbsp of the sautéed leek on each. Layer a slice of the fontina, half of the potatoes, half of the mushroom mixture, and a slice of the Gruyère on top. Finish with the remaining bread slices, buttered-side up. Be careful handling the uncooked sandwiches; there is a lot of stuff that may fall out as you move them. If it does, just tuck the fillings back inside.

8) Using a wide spatula, place both sandwiches in the pan, cover, and cook until the bottoms are nicely browned, about 4 minutes. Turn and cook until the second sides are browned and the cheese is melted, about 4 minutes longer.

9) Cut the sandwiches in half, if desired, and serve immediately.

MOSCONE
GRILLED CHEESE

SERVES 1

This sandwich with a Mediterranean motif is a tribute to Mayor George Moscone, considered a hero in San Francisco, who was assassinated along with gay rights icon and city supervisor Harvey Milk at San Francisco's City Hall in 1978. The fillings are a reference to Mayor Moscone's Italian heritage, and a spin on a traditional caprese salad (ripe tomato, torn basil, fresh mozzarella, and a drizzle of the best balsamic vinegar).

We make our own basil pesto and olive tapenade in big batches, handpicking two dozen bunches of fresh basil at a time, then mixing it with fragrant lavender buds. The store smells like heaven on pesto day. I encourage you to make your own fresh supply of these spreads as well—they're easier than you might think and they both keep well, so you can make a batch and use a little at a time.

1½ tsp salted butter, at room temperature

¼ tsp garlic powder

2 slices rustic artisan bread such as levain, sourdough, or white

1 Tbsp Kalamata Tapenade (page 156)

1 tsp Basil-Lavender Pesto (page 159)

2 slices Italian-style fontina cheese, preferably Fontina Val d'Aosta

2 or 3 slices ripe plum tomato (about ¼ in [6 mm] thick)

1 oz [30 g] fresh mozzarella cheese (see Note), thinly sliced

1) Heat a cast-iron or nonstick skillet over medium-low heat.

2) In a small bowl, stir together the butter and garlic powder until well blended.

3) Spread the garlic butter on one side of each bread slice, dividing it evenly. Place both slices, buttered-side down, on a clean cutting board. Spread the tapenade on one slice and the pesto on the other. Layer the fontina, tomato slices, and mozzarella on top of the tapenade. Finish with the pesto bread, buttered-side up.

4) Using a wide spatula, place the sandwich in the pan, cover, and cook until the bottom is nicely browned, about 4 minutes. Turn and cook until the second side is browned and the cheese is melted, about 4 minutes longer.

5) Cut the sandwich in half, if desired, and serve immediately.

NOTE: If you can find it, fresh *mozzarella di bufala* is especially good in this recipe. There are other cheese-making regions in the world making mozzarella from water buffalo's milk, but nothing compares to Italy's—it is a particularly rich and sweet mozzarella that makes an outstanding grilled cheese.

FETA FETISH
GRILLED CHEESE

SERVES 1

Feta is one of those cheeses people feel strongly about, like Limburger and Gorgonzola—they either love it or hate it. A really good fresh feta is sweet and salty, creamy and crumbly all at the same time, and a small amount will go a long way in adding flavor to a sandwich or salad. (Yes, that means I love it!) If you're a feta fan, too, total indulgence is one sandwich away.

If you have some extra feta, make yourself a traditional Greek salad to serve on the side. Just put chunks of tomato and cucumber, cubed feta, a handful of black olives, and a scattering of thin slices of red onion in a bowl. Toss with a drizzle of good olive oil, a squeeze of lemon juice, and a sprinkle of oregano.

1½ tsp salted butter, at room temperature

¼ tsp garlic powder

2 slices rustic artisan bread such as levain, sourdough, or white

2 slices Bel Paese or fontina cheese

2 or 3 slices ripe plum tomato (about ¼ in [6 mm] thick)

¼ cup [35 g] roasted red bell pepper strips (jarred or fresh), drained and patted dry with a paper towel

1 or 2 roasted or grilled eggplant slices (see Note)

Pinch of dried oregano

Pinch of red pepper flakes

Pinch of dried basil

2 Tbsp crumbled feta (we like Israeli sheep's-milk feta), drained

1) Heat a cast-iron or nonstick skillet over medium-low heat.

2) In a small bowl, stir together the butter and garlic powder until well blended.

3) Spread the garlic butter on one side of each bread slice, dividing it evenly. Place one slice, buttered-side down, on a clean cutting board. Layer the Bel Paese, tomato slices, bell pepper strips, and eggplant on top. Sprinkle the oregano, red pepper flakes, and basil on top of the eggplant, then top with the feta. Finish with the second slice of bread, buttered-side up. Be careful handling the uncooked sandwiches; there is a lot of stuff that may fall out as you move them. If it does, just tuck the fillings back inside.

4) Using a wide spatula, place the sandwich in the pan, cover, and cook until the bottom is nicely browned, about 4 minutes. Turn and cook until the second side is browned and the cheese is melted, about 4 minutes longer.

5) Cut the sandwich in half, if desired, and serve immediately.

NOTE: To roast or grill eggplant, trim off the stem of one small globe eggplant and cut lengthwise into ¼-in [6-mm] slices. Sprinkle both sides of the slices with kosher salt and lay flat on a baking sheet lined with paper towels for about 20 minutes. While the eggplant is resting, preheat the oven to 425°F [220°C], preheat a gas grill to high, or build a hot fire in a charcoal grill. The salt will draw water from the eggplant during this time; after it rests, pat the eggplant pieces dry with more paper towels. Line a baking sheet with parchment paper or aluminum foil or brush the grill rack with oil. Brush both sides of the eggplant slices with a light coating of olive oil. Arrange on the prepared baking sheet and roast in the oven until cooked through and lightly browned, about 15 minutes, or arrange on the hot grill grate and grill, turning once, until tender and nicely grill-marked, about 5 minutes per side. Use the extra eggplant for more sandwiches, or save for other uses such as an antipasto platter or baba ganoush. Can be frozen and thawed for later use.

Variation

Roasted Zucchini: Roasted zucchini is a nice addition to this sandwich. Slice one zucchini thinly lengthwise, then toss with a drizzle of olive oil and a pinch of salt and pepper and roast or grill alongside the eggplant. Use leftover roasted or grilled zucchini slices for an antipasto platter, or chop and add to scrambled eggs or stir-fries. The slices can be frozen and thawed for later use.

BLACK BEAN AND FRESH CORN
GRILLED CHEESE

SERVES 4

We once held an unusual grilled cheese contest: We invited members of the food press to the restaurant, where they were expecting us to demonstrate cooking techniques. Instead, we turned the tables and had them cook for us. We laid out more than fifty ingredients to choose from and had them design their own grilled cheese. The winning sandwich went on the menu, with sales going to the winner's charity of choice. This recipe was adapted from the winner, created by Amy Sherman, founder of the blog Cooking With Amy, based in San Francisco.

1 large ear fresh corn or ¾ cup [130 g] frozen corn kernels

½ fresh red or green jalapeño chile, seeded and cut into ¼-in [6-mm] dice (see Note)

½ fresh Hatch or Anaheim chile, seeded and cut into ¼-in [6-mm] dice (see Note)

½ cup [100 g] canned black beans, drained and rinsed

1 small ripe plum tomato, cut into ¼-in [6-mm] dice

¼ tsp ground cumin

¼ tsp garlic powder

¼ tsp kosher salt

¼ tsp freshly ground black pepper

2 Tbsp salted butter, at room temperature

½ tsp chipotle chile powder

8 slices sourdough bread

4 slices mild or medium Cheddar cheese

1 avocado, preferably Hass, pitted, peeled, and cut into slices about ¼ in [6 mm] thick (optional)

4 slices Oaxaca or Monterey Jack cheese

Pico de gallo or other salsa of your choice for serving (optional)

1) Husk the ear of corn and remove any corn silk. Cut the cob in half crosswise, put the halves cut-side down on a microwave-safe plate, and microwave on high for 2 minutes, or until the kernels turn just a shade darker and don't look raw (you may need to adjust the cooking time depending on the power of your microwave oven). Let the corn cool until easy to handle. Put both halves cut-side down on a cutting board and carefully slice off the kernels. Place the kernels in a medium bowl; discard the cobs. If using frozen corn, microwave in a medium bowl until warmed through and drain. Add the jalapeño and Hatch chiles to the bowl and toss to mix with the corn. Set aside.

2) In a small bowl, combine the black beans, tomato, cumin, garlic powder, salt, and black pepper and toss to mix well. Set aside. In another small bowl, stir together the butter and chipotle chile powder until well blended.

3) Heat a large cast-iron or nonstick skillet over medium-low heat.

4) Spread the chipotle butter on one side of each bread slice, dividing it evenly. Place one slice, buttered-side down, on a clean cutting board. Layer one slice of the Cheddar, one-fourth of the chile-corn mixture, one-fourth of the black bean mixture, a few slices of avocado (if using), and one slice of the Oaxaca cheese on top. Finish with a second slice of bread, buttered-side up. Repeat to assemble the remaining sandwiches.

5) Using a wide spatula, place as many sandwiches in the pan as will fit without crowding, cover, and cook until the bottoms are nicely browned, 2 to 3 minutes. Turn and cook until the second side is browned and the cheese is melted, 2 to 3 minutes longer.

6) Cut the sandwiches in half, if desired, and serve, with the *pico de gallo* on the side, if you like. Repeat to cook the remaining sandwiches.

NOTE: When adding hot chiles to your grilled cheese, keep in mind that the fat in the melted cheese cuts the heat of the chiles, so you will probably want to use hotter chiles than you think for the desired kick in the grilled sandwich. If you can get your hands on New Mexican Hatch chiles (which are only available for about 2 months of the year, during the summer), this is a wonderful way to get to know them. They are fairly mild (similar to jalapeños in heat) with a fruity, rich flavor. We like to use a mix of chiles in our recipes so no one flavor stands out. Remember, the heat of chiles can vary widely, so a cautious taste test is the only way to know how fiery a particular chile really is! See the Note on page 150 for more on how to handle chiles in the kitchen.

THE CATCH
GRILLED CHEESE

SERVES 2 TO 4

Nate and I love the San Francisco 49ers, and this sandwich refers to three memorable Niner moments.

The first is the winning touchdown reception by Dwight Clark, off a Joe Montana pass in the 1982 NFC Championship Game with the Dallas Cowboys, widely regarded as one of the most critical events in NFL history. It sent the 49ers to the Super Bowl (which they won!).

The second happened in 1999, during a playoff game with the Green Bay Packers. Forty-niner Terrell Owens caught a game-winning touchdown pass from quarterback Steve Young to cap a come-from-behind victory that broke a losing streak of five straight play-off losses to Green Bay.

Finally, in 2012, the Niners won another close playoff game against the New Orleans Saints. Quarter-back Alex Smith connected with Vernon Davis for a last-second touchdown that put the 49ers ahead.

It may be a bit of hubris, but, for us, this open-faced tuna melt is as memorable as these catches.

One 6-oz [170-g] can oil-packed tuna, drained

2 Tbsp mayonnaise

¼ Granny Smith apple, minced

½ celery stalk, minced

1 Tbsp minced fresh flat-leaf parsley

½ shallot, minced

1 garlic clove, minced

½ tsp kosher salt

½ tsp freshly ground black pepper

2 pretzel buns (hamburger size), split in half horizontally

4 tsp stone-ground mustard

8 slices ripe plum tomato (about ¼ in [6 mm] thick)

8 to 12 Bread 'n' Butter Pickles (page 147)

4 slices double-cream Gouda cheese

1) Preheat the oven to 450°F [230°C], with the convection option on, if you have it.

2) In a medium bowl, combine the tuna, mayonnaise, apple, celery, parsley, shallot, garlic, salt, and pepper and stir until well mixed. Set aside.

3) Place the pretzel bun halves on a baking sheet, cut-side up. Spread 1 tsp mustard on each bun half. Layer two tomato slices, two or three pickle chips, one-fourth of the tuna mixture, and one slice of the Gouda on top of each bun half.

4) Bake the open-faced sandwiches for about 3 minutes, or until the cheese is melted.

5) Cut each sandwich in half, if desired, and serve immediately.

FOGHORN LEGHORN
GRILLED CHEESE

SERVES 2

The Foghorn Leghorn Grilled Cheese is the result of two sources of inspiration: an extremely addictive and creamy Gorgonzola chicken gnocchi dish served at a little family-owned Italian joint in San Francisco; and customer requests for "something with chicken" and "something on whole wheat." You can use another kind of bread if you want, but a hearty whole-wheat bread, with just a touch of sweetness, really stands up to the pungent blue cheese and tangy dill mustard to make this sandwich, you know . . . crow.

2 tsp Dijon mustard

½ tsp dried dill

1 Tbsp salted butter, at room temperature

4 slices rustic artisan whole-wheat or whole-grain bread

4 slices Havarti cheese

4 oz [115 g] roasted chicken breast, from a good-quality market (see Note), thinly sliced

1 handful fresh baby arugula or baby spinach leaves

1 oz [30 g] crumbled Maytag or Point Reyes Farmstead blue cheese

1) Heat a cast-iron or nonstick skillet over medium-low heat.

2) In a small bowl, stir together the mustard and dill until well blended. Set aside.

3) Spread the butter on one side of each bread slice, dividing it evenly. Place two slices, buttered-side down, on a clean cutting board. Spread half of the dill mustard on each. Layer one slice of the Havarti, half of the chicken, half of the arugula, half of the blue cheese, and then another slice of the Havarti on top. Finish with the remaining bread slices, buttered-side up.

4) Using a wide spatula, place both sandwiches in the pan, cover, and cook until the bottoms are nicely browned, about 3 minutes. Turn and cook until the second sides are browned and the cheese is melted, about 3 minutes longer.

5) Cut the sandwiches in half, if desired, and serve immediately.

NOTE: You can use sautéed chicken breast in place of the deli sliced chicken in this sandwich. Start with a small (4- to 6-oz [115- to 170-g]) chicken breast, cut it carefully in half horizontally through the thickness to make two thinner fillets, and sprinkle with salt and pepper. Heat a nonstick skillet over medium-high heat, add 1 tsp vegetable oil, and swirl to coat the pan. Add the chicken slices and sauté for 3 minutes, then flip and sauté for another 3 minutes. Keep flipping every 3 minutes and cooking until the chicken is completely cooked through (you shouldn't see any pink when the breast is sliced) and lightly browned on the outside. If you have an instant-read thermometer, cook until the internal temperature reaches 165°F [74°C].

MOROCCAN CHICKEN
GRILLED CHEESE

SERVES 2

The Moroccan spice blend called *ras el hanout* was one of the inspirations for this unusual and sophisticated sandwich. The mixture is a mind-blowing combination of cinnamon, saffron, and other spices that magically renders everything it touches delicious. Admittedly, it's a bit of extra effort to prepare the components for this sandwich, and you can substitute store-bought ras el hanout and green olive tapenade for the homemade versions, if you wish. I use whole-wheat pitas or whole-wheat naan to stand in for *hobz belboula,* the traditional barley bread served with tagines in Morocco.

One 8-oz [230-g] boneless, skinless chicken breast

1 tsp Ras el Hanout (recipe follows)

¼ tsp kosher salt

1 tsp olive oil

1 Tbsp salted butter, at room temperature

2 whole-wheat pitas or whole-wheat naan breads, halved crosswise (not split)

¼ cup [55 g] Moroccan Green Olive, Artichoke, and Preserved Lemon Spread (page 158)

4 slices Mahón cheese

1) Heat a cast-iron or nonstick skillet over medium-high heat.

2) Rinse the chicken breast and pat dry with a paper towel. Cut the chicken breast in half horizontally through the thickness, so you have two equal-size fillets about ½ in [12 mm] thick. Sprinkle the ras el hanout and the salt on all sides of the chicken.

3) Swirl the olive oil in the hot skillet. Add the chicken slices and cook until opaque on the bottom, about 3 minutes. Turn and cook on the second side until the chicken is cooked through and you cannot see any pink in the middle, about 3 minutes longer. Transfer the chicken to a plate and let rest. Wipe out the skillet with a paper towel and set aside.

4) Spread the butter on one side of each piece of pita, dividing it evenly. Place two pieces, buttered-side down, on a clean cutting board. Spread each with half of the olive spread. Layer one slice of the Mahón, one piece of chicken, and another slice of the Mahón on top. Finish with the remaining pita pieces, buttered-side up.

5) Return the skillet to medium-low heat. Using a wide spatula, place both sandwiches in the pan, cover, and cook until the bottoms are nicely browned, about 3 minutes. Turn and cook until the second sides are browned and the cheese is melted, about 3 minutes longer.

6) Cut the sandwiches in half, if desired, and serve immediately.

RAS EL HANOUT

MAKES ABOUT ¼ CUP [30 G]

Ras el hanout, which translates as "top of the shop," is a spice mix prepared by merchants throughout Morocco. There is no standard formulation and merchants will guard the recipes for their proprietary blends. This is my favorite variation. Try sprinkling it on lamb, chicken, beef, or tofu before cooking.

1 Tbsp kosher salt

2 tsp ground ginger

2 tsp ground nutmeg

1½ tsp ground allspice

1½ tsp ground mace

1½ tsp ground cardamom

1½ tsp freshly ground black pepper

1 tsp ground cinnamon

1 tsp ground turmeric

25 saffron threads, crushed with the back of a spoon in a small bowl

Combine all of the ingredients in a small bowl and stir to mix thoroughly. Store in an airtight container in a cool, dark place for up to 3 months.

INDIAN LEFTOVERS
GRILLED CHEESE

SERVES 1

Leftovers of all kinds make great grilled cheeses, and Indian leftovers make one of the best. You can use almost any of your favorite Indian take-out dishes for this sandwich. If your chicken chunks are large, cut them into bite-size pieces. To make this vegetarian, use *bengan bartha, channa masala,* or *palak paneer* instead of the chicken. (What? No leftovers? It's fine to use store-bought naan and prepared Indian dishes from the grocery store instead.) Mint and cilantro chutney is the ubiquitous green sauce that comes with almost all take-out Indian food.

1½ tsp salted butter, at room temperature

1 naan bread, halved (not split)

1 tsp mint and cilantro chutney (optional)

2 slices pepper Jack cheese

⅓ cup [55 g] leftover chicken *tikka masala* or tandoori chicken

1) Heat a cast-iron or nonstick skillet over medium-low heat.

2) Spread the butter on one side of each piece of naan, dividing it evenly. Place one piece, buttered-side down, on a clean cutting board. Spread with the chutney (if using). Layer a slice of the pepper Jack, the chicken *tikka masala,* and the second slice of pepper Jack on top. Finish with the second piece of naan, buttered-side up.

3) Using a wide spatula, place the sandwich in the pan, cover, and cook until the bottom is nicely browned, about 3 minutes. Turn and cook until the second side is browned and the cheese is melted, about 3 minutes longer.

4) Cut the sandwich in half, if desired, and serve immediately.

BRO 'WICH PROJECT
GRILLED CHEESE

SERVES 1 HUNGRY BRO OR 2 NORMAL PEOPLE

One evening, one of our cooks decided to find out what would happen if he put *everything* on a sandwich—several cheeses, a few meats to match, sweet pickles and hot jalapeños, fresh crisp greens, and ripe tomato slices. . . . He could barely cram the results in his mouth, but we all had to try it—and then we asked if we could run it as a special. You can make all kinds of substitutions with this sandwich; whole-wheat or whole-grain breads work well, as do a variety of cheeses.

The name came from the sandwich's author himself; he joked about filming a spoof of *The Blair Witch Project* called *The Bro Witch Project* in San Francisco's Golden Gate Park. It would have a group of bros (frat-boy types) stumbling around the park at night, unable to find their way to the bars in the nearby Sunset District. We asked to repurpose the name for this sandwich, as it usually generates a response like "Whoa! Bro! Dude!" among those who witness its glory.

1½ tsp salted butter, at room temperature

3 slices sourdough or high-quality white bread

1 tsp Dijon mustard

1 slice Havarti cheese

1 slice roasted deli-style turkey

Scant handful of baby arugula or baby spinach leaves

2 strips thick-sliced bacon, cooked until crisp and drained

1 slice mild or medium Cheddar cheese

1 tsp stone-ground mustard

1 slice Colby Jack cheese

2 or 3 slices ripe plum tomato (about ¼ in [6 mm] thick)

3 or 4 Bread 'n' Butter Pickles (page 147)

1 slice black forest ham

1 slice Swiss cheese

1 Tbsp Pickled Red Onions (page 151)

3 or 4 slices fresh jalapeño chile (seeded if you like less heat) or Sweet Pickled Jalapeños (page 152)

1) Preheat the oven to 400°F [200°C], with the convection option on, if you have it. Place a baking sheet in the oven to preheat.

2) Spread the butter on one side of each bread slice, dividing it evenly. Place the slices, buttered-side down, on a clean cutting board. Spread the Dijon mustard on one slice, then top with the Havarti, turkey, arugula, bacon, and Cheddar. Spread the stone-ground mustard on the second slice of bread,

CONT'D

then layer with the Colby Jack, tomato slices, pickle chips, and ham. Place the Swiss on the third slice and arrange the pickled onions and jalapeño on top.

3) Remove the hot baking sheet from the oven and, using a wide spatula, carefully transfer the topped breads to the baking sheet. Bake for 3 to 4 minutes, until the cheeses start to melt and the fillings are warmed through. When you put the baking sheet in the oven, immediately begin to preheat a cast-iron or nonstick skillet over medium-low heat.

4) Using a wide spatula, transfer the topped breads to the hot skillet, bread-side down. Cook until the bottoms are nicely browned, about 2 minutes. Transfer to a clean cutting board.

5) Place the Swiss-jalapeño piece bread-side down on top of the piece with turkey and bacon, then carefully turn over the Colby Jack–ham piece and place it, bread-side up, on top of the sandwich.

6) Cut the sandwich very carefully into quarters and serve immediately.

CLUB TURKEY
GRILLED CHEESE

SERVES 2

We turned the classic turkey club sandwich into a grilled cheese, and thought it was so hip that it should have its own nightclub—introducing Club Turkey! Club sandwiches are classic, nostalgic Americana, featured on diner and country-club menus alike. Ours is not the traditional triple-decker, and we had to make some changes to make it work as a grilled cheese, like omitting the mayonnaise and substituting arugula for lettuce. We use two kinds of cheese—Cheddar and Havarti—to add complexity and variations in color and texture to the sandwich.

1 Tbsp salted butter, at room temperature

4 slices sourdough or white sandwich loaf

1 Tbsp stone-ground mustard

2 slices mild, medium, or sharp Cheddar or Colby cheese

6 oz [170 g] smoked turkey, thinly sliced

4 to 6 slices ripe plum tomato (about ¼ in [6 mm] thick)

1 handful baby arugula or baby spinach leaves

4 strips thick-sliced bacon, cooked until crisp and drained

2 slices Havarti or Monterey Jack cheese

1) Heat a cast-iron or nonstick skillet over medium-low heat.

2) Spread the butter on one side of each bread slice, dividing it evenly. Place two slices, buttered-side down, on a clean cutting board. Spread the mustard on each, again dividing it evenly. Layer one slice of the Cheddar, half of the turkey, two or three tomato slices, half of the arugula, two strips of bacon, and one slice of the Havarti on top. Finish with the remaining bread slices, buttered-side up.

3) Using a wide spatula, place both sandwiches in the pan, cover, and cook until the bottoms are nicely browned, about 3 minutes. Turn and cook until the second sides are browned and the cheese is melted, about 3 minutes longer.

4) Cut the sandwiches in half, if desired, and serve immediately.

Variations

Farmyard Club: Spread 1 Tbsp fresh chèvre on the second side of the buttered bread slices that are not spread with mustard.

Club Cluck or Club Oink: Substitute sliced roast chicken or ham for the smoked turkey.

WILD TURKEY
GRILLED CHEESE

SERVES 1

The Wild Turkey Grilled Cheese was one of the original sandwiches on our menu, so it holds a special place in our hearts. Smoky, sweet, tart, and rich at the same time, the bold flavors in this sandwich magically come together for a unique experience.

½ tsp olive oil

Scant handful of baby arugula leaves

Pinch of kosher salt

1½ tsp salted butter, at room temperature

2 slices rustic artisan bread such as levain, sourdough, or white

1 Tbsp red bell pepper and ancho chili jam (see Sources, page 168)

2 slices Havarti cheese

3 oz [85 g] smoked turkey, thinly sliced

1 Tbsp Pickled Red Onions (page 151)

1) Heat the olive oil in a small saucepan over medium heat. Add the arugula and salt and sauté for 15 seconds, or until the arugula is just beginning to wilt. Remove from the heat and set aside.

2) Heat a cast-iron or nonstick skillet over medium-low heat.

3) Spread the butter on one side of each bread slice, dividing it evenly. Place one slice, buttered-side down, on a clean cutting board. Spread with the jam. Layer one slice of the Havarti, the arugula, turkey, pickled onions, and the second slice of Havarti on top. Finish with the second slice of bread, buttered-side up.

4) Using a wide spatula, place the sandwich in the pan, cover, and cook until the bottom is nicely browned, about 3 minutes. Turn and cook until the second side is browned and the cheese is melted, about 3 minutes longer.

5) Cut the sandwich in half, if desired, and serve immediately.

THANKSGIVING LEFTOVERS
GRILLED CHEESE

SERVES 1

Here, I put the entire Thanksgiving meal between two slices of sage-buttered bread, which stands in for the stuffing. It's a great way to use up leftover Thanksgiving turkey, mashed potatoes, cranberry sauce, and gravy, but also a great excuse to roast a turkey breast, make some cranberry sauce and mashed potatoes, and give thanks in July, or any time.

1½ tsp salted butter, at room temperature

½ tsp minced fresh sage

2 slices rustic artisan whole-grain bread

2 slices Colby Jack cheese

2 Tbsp Cranberry Sauce (page 154)

¼ cup [55 g] Mashed Potatoes (see page 86)

3 oz [85 g] roasted turkey, thinly sliced

¼ cup [60 ml] Quick Cream Gravy (facing page; optional)

1) Heat a cast-iron or nonstick skillet over medium-low heat.

2) In a small bowl, stir together the butter and sage until well blended.

3) Spread the sage butter on one side of each bread slice, dividing it evenly. Place one slice, buttered-side down, on a clean cutting board. Layer one slice of the Colby Jack, the cranberry sauce, mashed potatoes, turkey, and the second slice of Colby Jack on top. Finish with the second slice of bread, buttered-side up.

4) Using a wide spatula, place the sandwich in the pan, cover, and cook until the bottom is nicely browned, about 3 minutes. Turn and cook until the second side is browned and the cheese is melted, about 3 minutes longer.

5) Cut the sandwich in half, if desired, and serve immediately, with the gravy on the side for dipping, if you like.

QUICK CREAM GRAVY

MAKES ABOUT 1⅓ CUPS [320 ML]

The sage in this gravy gives it just the right flavor to complement the Thanksgiving Leftovers Grilled Cheese. Try it—you'll see!

2 Tbsp salted butter, at room temperature

3 Tbsp all-purpose flour

1 cup [240 ml] heavy cream

Kosher salt and freshly ground black pepper

½ tsp minced fresh sage or ¼ tsp dried rubbed sage (optional)

1 to 3 Tbsp milk, if needed

1) Melt the butter in a small saucepan over medium-low heat. Gradually whisk in the flour until combined, and then cook, whisking constantly, for about 30 seconds.

2) Gradually add the cream to the butter mixture, still whisking constantly, until the mixture is smooth. Whisk in ½ tsp salt, ½ tsp pepper, and the sage (if using). Break up any lumps. Cook, whisking occasionally, for about 5 minutes, or until the gravy thickens. Taste and adjust the seasoning with more salt and pepper, if needed. If the gravy is too thick, thin it by whisking in a little milk, 1 Tbsp at a time, until you reach the desired consistency.

3) Store in an airtight container in the refrigerator for up to 3 days. Rewarm in a microwave or over low heat in a small saucepan before serving.

JALAPEÑO POPPER
GRILLED CHEESE

SERVES 1

The Jalapeño Popper Grilled Cheese really should be called "The Scout." One night while recipe testing, Nate and I fed our friend Scout—who was also the very first customer at our restaurant—a goat cheese and Jack grilled cheese. Scout's response: "This is good, but can I put some jalapeños on it?" Thus it dawned on us that the jalapeño popper, that mainstay of sports bars everywhere, was a perfect candidate for grilled cheesification.

1½ tsp salted butter, room temperature

2 slices rustic artisan bread such as levain, sourdough, or white

1 Tbsp fresh chèvre (goat cheese), at room temperature

1 slice Monterey Jack cheese

¼ cup [55 g] Apricot-Jalapeño Relish (page 155)

2 strips thick-sliced bacon, cooked until crisp and drained

1) Heat a cast-iron or nonstick skillet over medium-low heat.

2) Spread the butter on one side of each bread slice, dividing it evenly. Place both slices, buttered-side down, on a clean cutting board. Spread the chèvre on one slice and place the Jack on the other. Carefully spread the relish on top of the Jack and place the bacon on top of the relish. Finish with the second slice of bread, chèvre-side down.

3) Using a wide spatula, place the sandwich in the pan, cover, and cook until the bottom is nicely browned, about 3 minutes. Turn and cook until the second side is browned and the cheese is melted, about 3 minutes longer.

4) Cut the sandwich in half, if desired, and serve immediately.

PIGLET
GRILLED CHEESE

SERVES 1

An irresistible version of the ham-and-cheese sandwich, the Piglet has been on our menu since Day One. The inspiration came from a simple farmer-style cheese plate: fresh apples, a slab of herb bread, shavings of ham, stone-ground mustard, and a wedge of aged Cheddar. The most popular addition with our customers is roasted tomatoes, and some folks prefer deli-style roasted turkey to the ham.

1½ tsp salted butter, at room temperature

¼ tsp minced fresh rosemary or ⅛ tsp dried rosemary, crumbled

2 slices rustic artisan bread such as levain, sourdough, or white

1 Tbsp Apple Mustard (page 160)

2 slices medium or sharp Cheddar cheese

2 oz [55 g] thinly sliced cured ham

1) Heat a cast-iron or nonstick skillet over medium-low heat.

2) In a small bowl, stir together the butter and rosemary until well blended.

3) Spread the rosemary butter on one side of each bread slice, dividing it evenly. Place one slice, buttered-side down, on a clean cutting board. Spread with the apple mustard. Layer one slice of the Cheddar, the ham, and the second slice of Cheddar on top. Finish with the second slice of bread, buttered-side up.

4) Using a wide spatula, place the sandwich in the pan, cover, and cook until the bottom is nicely browned, about 3 minutes. Turn and cook until the second side is browned and the cheese is melted, about 3 minutes longer.

5) Cut the sandwich in half, if desired, and serve immediately.

HAWAIIAN
GRILLED CHEESE

SERVES 2

Hawaiian pizza is one of our guilty pleasures—gooey mozzarella, sweet-tart pineapple, savory ham, and spicy tomato sauce . . . aloha mmmm. We turned this classic pizza combination into one heck of a grilled cheese sandwich by using fresh, high-quality ingredients and adding a splash of love.

4 slices fresh pineapple (about ¼ in [6 mm] thick), cored, or ½ of a small can of pineapple rings in juice, drained

6 to 8 slices ripe plum tomato (about ¼ in [6 mm] thick)

1 Tbsp salted butter, at room temperature

4 slices Hawaiian bread (slightly sweet white bread) or artisan white bread

4 slices [85 g] fontina cheese

4 oz [115 g] sliced ham

3 oz [85 g] fresh mozzarella cheese, thinly sliced

Pinch of red repper flakes (optional)

1) Preheat the oven to 375°F [190°C]. Line a baking sheet with parchment paper or aluminum foil.

2) Arrange the pineapple and tomato slices on the prepared baking sheet and bake for 12 minutes, or until the surfaces appear dry but not yet browned, turning the pieces over halfway through. Remove from the oven and set aside.

3) Heat a cast-iron or nonstick skillet over medium-low heat.

4) Spread the butter on one side of each bread slice, dividing it evenly. Place two slices, buttered-side down, on a clean cutting board. Layer two slices of the fontina, half of the ham, three or four slices of roasted tomato, two rings of roasted pineapple, and half of the mozzarella on top of each. Sprinkle with the red pepper flakes (if using). Finish with the remaining slices of bread, buttered-side up.

5) Using a wide spatula, place both sandwiches in the pan, cover, and cook until the bottoms are nicely browned, about 4 minutes. Turn and cook until the second sides are browned, the cheese is melted, and the other ingredients are heated through, about 4 minutes longer.

6) Cut the sandwiches in half, if desired, and serve immediately.

CUBANO
GRILLED CHEESE

SERVES 6

The Cubano, the aptly named national sandwich of Cuba, has seen a thousand variations on its tasty basics, which are ham, roasted pork, pickles, Swiss cheese, and mustard, traditionally on a soft roll. My version features house-made pulled pork slathered in a rich coffee rub, cured artisanal ham, two kinds of cheese, sweet pickled red onions, and our famous (and so easy!) bread 'n' butter pickles. We trade the traditional soft roll for rustic, crusty bread for optimal buttery crunch.

This sandwich takes a bit of planning ahead and prep work, but it's worth it. If you have pulled pork left over, save the pan juices to make delicious Pulled Pork Stew (page 115) or stir ½ cup [85 g] or so of pulled pork into Basic Mac 'n' Cheese (page 120). And of course you can always pile it on a soft hamburger bun with some Kale Slaw (page 163), a few Bread 'n' Butter Pickles, and a slather of BBQ sauce for an ever-popular classic pulled pork sandwich.

If you don't want to go through the hassle of making your own pulled pork, pick some up at your favorite BBQ joint.

DRY RUB

1 Tbsp finely ground espresso beans or instant espresso powder

¼ cup [30 g] *pimentón* (smoked paprika)

2 Tbsp kosher salt

1½ Tbsp freshly ground black pepper

1 Tbsp sugar

1 Tbsp chili powder

1½ tsp garlic powder

½ tsp cayenne pepper

2 lb [910 g] pork shoulder (also called pork butt or Boston butt), trimmed of any large visible chunks of fat

2 to 4 cups [480 to 960 ml] apple juice (see Note)

3 Tbsp salted butter, at room temperature

1½ tsp garlic powder

12 slices rustic artisan bread such as levain, sourdough, or white

3 Tbsp stone-ground mustard

6 slices Emmenthaler or Swiss cheese

6 oz [170 g] thinly sliced ham

6 Tbsp Pickled Red Onions (page 151)

18 to 24 Bread 'n' Butter Pickles (page 147)

6 slices Muenster cheese

1) Preheat the oven to 375°F [190°C].

2) To make the dry rub: In a small bowl, combine the espresso, *pimentón,* salt, black pepper, sugar, chili powder, garlic powder, and cayenne pepper and stir to mix well.

3) Rub the pork thoroughly with the dry rub, coating it thickly on all sides. Place the pork in a Dutch oven or ovenproof saucepan deep enough so the pan can be covered without touching the meat. Pour in enough of the apple juice to come halfway up the sides of the pork. Cover the pan tightly with one layer of plastic wrap and then one or two layers of aluminum foil (don't worry, the plastic wrap will be fine in the oven; we want this airtight!). Bake for 3 to 4 hours, or until the pork is falling-apart tender; a fork should move easily through to the center of the meat. Pour off any remaining juices in the pan and let the pork cool in the pan for 10 minutes.

4) Using your hands or two forks, shred the pork into bite-size chunks. Measure off 3 cups [510 g] for your Cubanos. (Store the remainder in an airtight container in the refrigerator for up to 3 days; our favorite use is snacking.)

5) Heat a cast-iron or nonstick skillet over medium-low heat.

6) In a small bowl, stir together the butter and garlic powder until well blended.

7) Spread the garlic butter on one side of each bread slice, dividing it evenly. Place two slices, buttered-side down, on a clean cutting board. Spread ½ Tbsp of the mustard on each. Layer a slice of the Emmenthaler, one-sixth of the ham, 1 Tbsp of the pickled onions, 3 or 4 pickles, ½ cup [85 g] of the pulled pork, and a slice of the Muenster on top of each. Finish with two slices of bread, buttered-side up.

8) Using a wide spatula, place both sandwiches in the pan, cover, and cook until the bottoms are nicely browned, about 4 minutes. Turn and cook until the second sides are browned and the cheese is melted, about 4 minutes longer. Repeat, assembling and cooking the remaining four sandwiches.

9) Cut the sandwiches in half, if desired, and serve immediately.

NOTE: We use fresh organic apple juice. You can also use cola, Dr Pepper, or orange juice for a slightly different flavor.

TRUFFLED GRILLED CHEESE
WITH BACON AND CHIVES

SERVES 2 AS A MAIN DISH OR 4 AS AN APPETIZER

Sometimes I like to put together special tasting menus; and when I include this sandwich, it is always a hit. It's very rich, so it's best enjoyed in small doses as a decadent appetizer or snack. It's even better paired with a glass of chilled brut Champagne.

The best part is that the truffled cheese browns and crisps in the holes of the bread as it cooks on the griddle; the effect is amazing. Be patient and don't move the sandwich around the pan while it's cooking. Once you taste that crusty cheese, you'll know what I mean.

1 Tbsp salted butter, at room temperature

4 slices ciabatta

4 slices Boschetto al Tartufo or other semisoft truffled cheese

4 strips thick-sliced bacon, cooked until crisp and drained

2 Tbsp crème fraîche

1 tsp truffle oil

6 fresh chives, minced

1) Heat a cast-iron or nonstick skillet over medium-low heat.

2) Spread the butter on one side of each bread slice, dividing it evenly. Place two slices, buttered-side down, on a clean cutting board. Layer one slice of the Boschetto al Tartufo, two strips of the bacon, and then a second slice of the cheese on top of each. Finish with the remaining slices of bread, buttered-side up.

3) Using a wide spatula, place both sandwiches in the pan, cover, and cook until the bottoms are nicely browned, about 2 minutes. Turn and cook until the cheese melts through the holes of the ciabatta on the bottoms and is lightly browned, about 2 minutes longer.

4) Cut each sandwich in half for an entrée; or into quarters for an appetizer. Top each piece with a dollop of crème fraîche, a drizzle of truffle oil, and a sprinkle of chives and serve immediately.

BUTTERNUT BUSTER
GRILLED CHEESE

SERVES 2

This hit sandwich is named after legendary San Francisco Giants catcher Buster Posey, who led the team to their World Series Championship in 2012. Our flagship location is two blocks from the Giants' stadium, so before every ball game we are swarmed with fans bedecked in the Giants' colors: (butternut) orange and black. Inspired by classic Italian squash ravioli with sage and brown butter, we recommend making this sandwich in playoffs season—fall, that is—or winter, when butternut squash is in season.

Idiazábal is a lovely hard sheep's-milk cheese from the Basque region; if you can't find it, substitute a good-quality, nutty Gruyère. Use the remaining roasted squash (and any extra fresh sage) to make the delicious Butternut Squash Soup on page 108. You could also cut it into cubes for pretty fall salads, or mash it up for a side dish.

1 small butternut squash, peeled, halved lengthwise, and seeds and strings removed

1 Tbsp olive oil

Kosher salt and freshly ground black pepper

1½ tsp vegetable oil

½ small yellow onion, cut into ¼-in [6-mm] dice

1 Tbsp salted butter, at room temperature

4 slices rustic artisan bread such as levain, sourdough, or white

8 fresh sage leaves

2 slices Italian-style fontina cheese, preferably Fontina Val d'Aosta

2 oz [55 g] thinly sliced prosciutto or speck

1 oz [25 g] Idiazábal cheese, grated

1) Preheat the oven to 375°F [190°C]. Line a baking sheet with parchment paper or aluminum foil and coat well with nonstick cooking spray.

2) Cut the squash into slices about ¼ in [6 mm] thick. Pile the squash on the prepared baking sheet, drizzle with the olive oil, and sprinkle with a pinch each of salt and pepper. Toss to coat well and spread the squash slices to lie flat in a single layer on the baking sheet. Roast for 15 to 20 minutes, or until easily pierced with a fork and just beginning to brown. (If the squash begins to brown before softening, sprinkle with water and cover with foil.) Transfer to a wire rack and let cool on the pan. Set aside four of the cooked squash slices and store the rest for another use.

3) While the squash is roasting, warm the vegetable oil in a small skillet over low heat. Add the onion and a pinch of salt and stir to combine. Cover and cook, stirring every couple of minutes, until the onion is translucent and soft, about 8 minutes. Uncover, raise the heat to medium, and cook, stirring often to prevent scorching, until the onion is the color of light brown sugar, about 5 minutes longer. Remove from the heat and set aside.

4) Heat a cast-iron or nonstick skillet over medium-low heat.

5) Spread the butter on one side of each bread slice, dividing it evenly. Place two slices, buttered-side up, on a clean cutting board. Carefully lay four of the sage leaves on each piece in a star pattern and, using your fingers, smear a little butter over the sage stars to hold them in place during cooking. Set aside on a corner of the cutting board.

6) Place the remaining bread, buttered-side down, on the cutting board. Layer half of the caramelized onions, one slice of the fontina, half of the reserved cooked squash, half of the prosciutto, and half of the Idiazábal on top of each. Finish with the decorated breads, sage stars facing up.

7) Using a wide spatula, place both sandwiches in the pan with the sage stars facing down, cover, and cook until the bottoms are nicely browned, about 4 minutes. Turn and cook until the second sides are browned and the cheese is melted, about 4 minutes longer.

8) Cut the sandwiches in half, if desired, and serve immediately, with the sage stars facing up.

DON GONDOLA
GRILLED CHEESE

SERVES 1

Long live the Don! Don Gondola is the stage name of a talented accordion player with a penchant for wild costumes and even wilder stage antics. When the Don rolls through San Francisco, we always host a live accordion show at one of our stores in his honor. So play some polka and sing along at the top of your lungs while you make his signature sandwich.

1½ tsp salted butter, at room temperature

¼ tsp garlic powder

2 slices Italian loaf

1 tsp Basil-Lavender Pesto (page 159)

2 slices provolone cheese (young, plain provolone, not aged or smoked)

2 oz [55 g] thinly sliced salami (we like *salume finocchiona,* a Tuscan salami made with fennel)

2 or 3 slices small ripe plum tomato (about ¼ in [6 mm] thick)

1) Heat a cast-iron or nonstick skillet over medium-low heat.

2) In a small bowl, stir together the butter and garlic powder until well blended.

3) Spread the garlic butter on one side of each bread slice, dividing it evenly. Place one slice, buttered-side down, on a clean cutting board. Spread with the pesto. Layer one slice of the provolone, the salami, tomato slices, and then the second slice of provolone on top. Finish with the second slice of bread, buttered-side up.

4) Using a wide spatula, place the sandwich in the pan, cover, and cook until the bottom is nicely browned, 3 to 4 minutes. Turn and cook until the second side is browned and the cheese is melted, about 3 minutes longer.

5) Cut the sandwich in half, if desired, and serve immediately.

PIZZA-WICH
GRILLED CHEESE

SERVES 2

Because I'm obsessed with all things that involve bread and cheese, I put some effort into learning how to make great Neapolitan-style pizzas at home. Along the way, I developed a simple, foolproof marinara pizza sauce that comes together in seconds. I think I like it even more in this pizza-flavored grilled cheese. You will have extra sauce; you could invite some friends over for a Pizza-wich party, letting everyone put their favorite pizza toppings in their sandwich, or save the extra and toss it with fresh pasta and a bit of freshly grated Parmesan for a super-easy supper the next day.

One 14-oz [400-g] can Italian whole peeled tomatoes, preferably San Marzano, drained

3½ tsp olive oil

½ tsp red wine vinegar

1 garlic clove, minced

½ tsp kosher salt

½ tsp dried oregano, crumbled

4 slices Italian loaf

2 Tbsp freshly grated Parmesan cheese, preferably Parmigiano-Reggiano

2 oz [55 g] pepperoni, thinly sliced (optional)

3 oz [85 g] fresh mozzarella, thinly sliced

Red pepper flakes for sprinkling (optional)

1) In a food processor fitted with the metal blade or in a blender, combine the tomatoes, 1½ tsp of the olive oil, the vinegar, garlic, salt, and oregano. Process until the sauce is smooth and no chunks remain, about 10 seconds. Scrape the tomato sauce into a small bowl and set aside.

2) Heat a cast-iron or nonstick skillet over medium-low heat.

3) Brush one side of each bread slice with the remaining 2 tsp olive oil. Place two slices, oiled-side down, on a clean cutting board. Sprinkle half of the Parmesan on each. Then, spread 2 Tbsp of the tomato sauce over the Parmesan. Layer half of the pepperoni (if using) and half of the mozzarella on top. Sprinkle with the red pepper flakes (if using). Finish with the remaining slices of bread, oiled-side up.

4) Using a wide spatula, place both sandwiches in the pan, cover, and cook until the bottoms are nicely browned, 3 to 4 minutes. Turn and cook until the second sides are browned and the cheese is melted, about 3 minutes longer.

5) Cut the sandwiches in half, if desired, and serve immediately, with extra tomato sauce on the side for dipping if you like.

MUFFALETTA
GRILLED CHEESE

SERVES 1

The muffaletta (also spelled muffuletta and probably twenty other ways, but generally pronounced "moo-fuh-LET-uh") originated in the French Quarter of New Orleans. Traditionally made on a light flat roll that is also called a muffaletta, it's a staple at lunch counters throughout Louisiana. While muffalettas are usually assembled and allowed to sit, wrapped, for several hours in a refrigerator before eating to allow the flavors to meld, we cook ours right away so that the bread can crisp up as a grilled cheese should.

1½ tsp salted butter, at room temperature

One 4-in [10-cm] square of focaccia bread, split through the thickness (plain, rosemary, or herb focaccia all work equally well)

1 slice provolone cheese (young, plain provolone, not aged or smoked)

2 or 3 slices small ripe plum tomato (about ¼ in [6 mm] thick)

2 thin slices mortadella

1 slice smoked mozzarella cheese (also called Scamorza)

2 thin slices capicola

4 thin slices dry salami

2 Tbsp Muffaletta Olive Salad (page 157)

1 slice Jarlsberg cheese

1) Heat a cast-iron or nonstick skillet over medium-low heat.

2) Spread the butter on the outside of each piece of focaccia, dividing it evenly. Place the bottom half, buttered-side down, on a clean cutting board. Layer the provolone, tomato slices, mortadella, mozzarella, capicola, salami, olive salad, and Jarlsberg on top. Finish with the top half of the bread, buttered-side up.

3) Using a wide spatula, place the sandwich in the pan, cover, and cook until the bottom is nicely browned, 3 to 4 minutes. Turn and cook until the second side is browned and the cheese is melted, about 3 minutes longer.

4) Cut the sandwich in half, if desired, and serve immediately.

ROAST BEEF AND BLUE CHEESE
GRILLED CHEESE

SERVES 1

Warm savory roast beef and salty pungent blue cheese give this grilled cheese its name; the purple-black, sweet and acidic Balsamic Onion Marmalade ties everything together. This is a grown-up grilled cheese and these are strong flavors, but so good together. If you don't want to take the time to make the marmalade, you can substitute store-bought onion jam, but don't skip it altogether—it takes this sandwich over the top.

1½ tsp salted butter, at room temperature

2 slices white country bread

2 Tbsp Balsamic Onion Marmalade (page 161)

2 slices Muenster cheese

3 oz [85 g] thinly sliced roast beef

1½ Tbsp crumbled blue cheese (we especially like King Island Dairy's Roaring Forties Blue from Australia and New Zealand for this sandwich; see Note)

1) Heat a cast-iron or nonstick skillet over medium-low heat.

2) Spread the butter on one side of each bread slice, dividing it evenly. Place one slice, buttered-side down, on a clean cutting board. Spread with the onion marmalade. Layer one slice of the Muenster, the roast beef, blue cheese, and the second slice of Muenster on top. Finish with the second slice of bread, buttered-side up.

3) Using a wide spatula, place the sandwich in the pan, cover, and cook until the bottom is nicely browned, 3 to 4 minutes. Turn and cook until the second side is browned and the cheese is melted, about 3 minutes longer.

4) Cut the sandwich in half, if desired, and serve immediately.

NOTE: The sharpness of blue cheeses can vary considerably; some are creamy and mild, some so sharp you can smell them across the room the minute they're unwrapped. You may want to adjust the amount you add to this sandwich depending on the strength of the cheese you select as well as your own tastes.

WINDY CITY
GRILLED CHEESE

SERVES 2

Chicago is famous for many things, including its lake-shore, architecture, long-winded politicians, deep-dish pizza, and a sandwich called the Italian Beef. The classic version features hot roast beef and a pickled vegetable relish called *giardiniera*. Nate, who grew up in Chicago, had the brilliant idea of turning that roast beast into a grilled cheese.

We make our own giardiniera for the restaurant, dicing the veggies small so that the chunks can be distributed evenly in the sandwiches, and we include our recipe in this book. But if you are lucky enough to find a good-quality jar of this delicious condiment (try your local Italian specialty-foods store), you are welcome to use that instead; just chop it before using.

1 Tbsp salted butter, at room temperature

½ tsp garlic powder

4 slices rustic artisan bread such as levain, sourdough, or white

4 slices provolone cheese

6 oz [170 g] thinly sliced roast beef

⅓ cup [75 g] Giardiniera (page 149), drained

1) Heat a cast-iron or nonstick skillet over medium-low heat.

2) In a small bowl, stir together the butter and garlic powder until well blended.

3) Spread the garlic butter on one side of each bread slice, dividing it evenly. Place two slices, buttered-side down, on a clean cutting board. Layer one slice of the provolone, half of the roast beef, half of the giardiniera, and another slice of the provolone on top of each. Finish with the remaining slices of bread, buttered-side up.

4) Using a wide spatula, place both sandwiches in the pan and cook until the bottoms are nicely browned, about 4 minutes. Turn and cook until the second sides are browned and the cheese is melted, about 4 minutes longer.

5) Cut the sandwiches in half, if desired, and serve immediately.

AMERICAN DIP
GRILLED CHEESE

SERVES 2

The origin of this sandwich is probably pretty obvious. I just took a classic, old-fashioned "fancy" meal and turned it into a grilled cheese. If you cannot find garlic or herb Jack, try sprinkling ½ tsp garlic powder on the potato slices before roasting; a little punch of garlic in this sandwich is divine.

1 small Yukon gold potato, scrubbed but not peeled, cut into slices about ¼ in [6 mm] thick

½ tsp olive oil

Kosher salt and freshly ground black pepper

1 Tbsp salted butter, at room temperature

4 fresh chives, minced

¼ cup [55 g] crème fraîche, sour cream, or plain Greek yogurt

2 Tbsp prepared horseradish, not cream style

4 slices rustic artisan bread such as levain, sourdough, or white

4 slices garlic or herb Jack cheese

6 oz [170 g] thinly sliced roast beef

1) Preheat the oven to 425°F [220°C]. Line a baking sheet with parchment paper or aluminum foil.

2) In a bowl, combine the potato slices with the olive oil and a pinch each of salt and pepper and toss gently until the potatoes are evenly coated. Spread the potatoes in a single layer on the prepared baking sheet and roast until cooked through and starting to brown in spots, about 15 minutes. Set aside.

3) In a small bowl, stir together the butter and chives until well blended. In another small bowl, stir together the crème fraîche and horseradish until well combined. Set both bowls aside. (Store, covered tightly with plastic wrap, in the refrigerator for up to 3 days.)

4) Heat a cast-iron or nonstick skillet over medium-low heat.

5) Spread the chive butter on one side of each bread slice, dividing it evenly. Place two slices, buttered-side down, on a clean cutting board. Layer one slice of the Jack, half of the roast beef, three or four potato slices, and then another slice of the Jack on top of each. Finish with the remaining slices of bread, buttered-side up.

6) Using a wide spatula, place both sandwiches in the pan, cover, and cook until the bottoms are nicely browned, about 4 minutes. Turn and cook until the second sides are browned and the cheese is melted, about 4 minutes longer.

7) Cut the sandwiches in half, if desired, and serve with the horseradish cream on the side for dipping.

ST. PATRICK'S DAY
GRILLED CHEESE

SERVES 4

Everyone is Irish on St. Patrick's Day, and the grilled cheeses need to be Irish, too. One March afternoon, I took the leftovers from a traditional St. Patrick's Day feast—corned beef and cabbage with potatoes and fresh Irish soda bread—and spent an afternoon in the test kitchen. *Sláinte!* (Cheers!) Of course you can make it into a grilled cheese. And a darn tasty one at that. I recommend serving this with a pint of Guinness, of course.

BRAISED CABBAGE

¼ small head green cabbage, stem portion removed, separated into leaves

1½ cups [360 ml] beer, preferably Guinness or other dark Irish beer

1 Tbsp kosher salt

MASHED POTATOES

1 medium Yukon gold potato, peeled and cut into ½-in [12-mm] cubes

1 tsp kosher salt

2 tsp salted butter, at room temperature

1 Tbsp whole milk or cream

1 Tbsp prepared horseradish, not cream style (optional)

2 Tbsp salted butter, at room temperature

8 slices Irish Soda Bread (page 88)

4 tsp stone-ground mustard

8 slices porter Cheddar or Irish Cheddar cheese

12 oz [340 g] cooked, thinly sliced corned beef

1) To make the cabbage: In a small saucepan over medium heat, combine the cabbage, beer, and salt. Stir to mix and bring to a boil. Stir again, cover loosely, and lower the heat so the beer is simmering gently. Cook, stirring occasionally, until the cabbage is tender, about 20 minutes. Remove from the heat, drain the cabbage, and set aside.

2) Meanwhile, make the mashed potatoes: Place the potato and salt in a small saucepan and add cold water to just cover. Bring to a boil over medium heat, then lower the heat to maintain a gentle simmer. Cover and cook for about 10 minutes, or until the potato is soft and beginning to fall apart. Remove from the heat, drain, and then add the hot potato to a stand mixer fitted with the paddle attachment or to a medium bowl with a handheld mixer. Add the butter and milk and blend on medium speed just until smooth, 20 to 30 seconds. Be careful not to overbeat and don't worry about getting your mashed potatoes perfectly smooth; some chunks are fine. Stir in the horseradish (if using) and set aside.

3) Heat a cast-iron or nonstick skillet over medium-low heat.

4) Spread the butter on one side of each bread slice, dividing it evenly. Place two slices, buttered-side down, on a clean cutting board. Spread 1 tsp of the mustard on each. Layer one slice of the Cheddar, ¼ cup [55 g] of the mashed potatoes, one-fourth of the corned beef, two leaves (cut to approximately the size of the bread) of the braised cabbage, and then a second slice of Cheddar on top. Finish with two slices of bread, buttered-side up.

5) Using a wide spatula, place both sandwiches in the pan, cover, and cook until the bottoms are nicely browned, about 3 minutes. Turn and cook until the second sides are browned and the cheese is melted, about 3 minutes longer. Repeat, assembling and cooking the remaining two sandwiches.

6) Cut the sandwiches in half, if desired, and serve immediately.

IRISH SODA BREAD

MAKES 1 LOAF

Traditional Irish soda bread is so easy to make and so wonderful when it's fresh. It's usually formed into a round and baked on a baking sheet, but we bake ours in a loaf pan so it's easier to slice into sandwich slices. We like to make it as part of an Irish dinner and then use the left-overs the next day for St. Patrick's Day Grilled Cheese.

3½ cups [445 g] all-purpose flour (see Note)

¼ cup [50 g] granulated sugar

1 tsp baking soda

1½ tsp kosher salt

2 Tbsp caraway seeds (optional, but highly recommended)

1 egg

1 cup [240 ml] buttermilk (see Note)

¼ cup [45 g] dried currants or raisins (optional)

1) Preheat the oven to 400°F [220°C]. Butter a 9-by-5-in [23-by-12-cm] loaf pan and set aside.

2) In a large bowl, stir together the flour, sugar, baking soda, salt, and caraway seeds (if using) with a whisk and set aside. In a small bowl, whisk the egg to blend and then whisk in the buttermilk. Add the buttermilk mixture and currants (if using) to the flour mixture and stir with a wooden spoon until the dough is shaggy but no floury streaks remain, about 1 minute. Scrape the dough onto a floured cutting board or work surface and knead for about 1 minute, until the dough comes together in a ball. (The dough will be sticky, so add flour to the board and your hands as needed.) Pat the dough into an oblong shape about the same length as the loaf pan and then place the dough in the pan. Cut a slit about 1 in [2.5 cm] deep down the center of the loaf with a sharp knife.

3) Bake for 15 minutes, then lower the oven temperature to 375°F [190°C] and bake for about 20 minutes longer, or until the top is evenly browned and the loaf sounds hollow when you tilt it out of the pan and tap it on the bottom. Let cool completely to room temperature before slicing. Wrap any unused bread tightly and store at room temperature for up to 2 days or freeze for up to 1 month, warming in a 350°F [180°C] oven for 10 to 12 minutes before serving.

NOTES: You can substitute stone-ground whole-wheat flour for up to one-third of the all-purpose flour in this recipe.

If you don't have buttermilk on hand, you can "sour" regular milk by adding 2 tsp white vinegar or lemon juice to a measuring cup and then adding whole milk to equal 1 cup [240 ml]. Stir and let sit for 1 minute before using. Don't be alarmed; the milk will curdle slightly.

REUBENESQUE
GRILLED CHEESE

SERVES 1

Grilled cheese, meet Reuben. Reuben, meet grilled cheese. The only secret here is to use the highest-quality ingredients you can find. We use pastrami on ours, but a traditional Reuben sandwich can be invoked by substituting corned beef. Swiss is the cheese of choice here, but I like the extra flavor added by Gruyère, so I use both. This is a grilled cheese, after all.

Oh, and for the Reuben traditionalists, we leave off the Russian dressing—there's enough going on without it, and it makes the sandwich extra messy. But if you rue the absence, just mix together 1 tsp ketchup and 1 tsp mayonnaise in a small bowl and spread it on the inside of the top piece of bread.

1½ tsp salted butter, at room temperature

2 slices light rye bread (see Note)

1½ tsp stone-ground mustard

1 slice Gruyère cheese

3 oz [85 g] thinly sliced pastrami

2 Tbsp sauerkraut, drained and patted dry with a paper towel

4 Bread 'n' Butter Pickles (page 147)

1 slice Jarlsberg or Emmenthaler cheese

1) Heat a cast-iron or nonstick skillet over medium-low heat.

2) Spread the butter on one side of each bread slice, dividing it evenly. Place one slice, buttered-side down, on a clean cutting board. Spread with the mustard. Layer the Gruyère, pastrami, sauerkraut, pickle chips, and Jarlsberg on top. Finish with the second slice of bread, buttered-side up.

3) Using a wide spatula, place the sandwich in the pan, cover, and cook until the bottom is nicely browned, about 3 minutes. Turn and cook until the second side is browned and the cheese is melted, 3 to 4 minutes longer.

4) Cut the sandwich in half, if desired, and serve immediately.

NOTE: You can use dark rye bread in this recipe, but the higher percentage of rye flour makes the bread more crumbly when toasted, and you may need a knife and fork.

GRILLED CHEESE
BIRTHDAY CAKE

SERVES 15 TO 20

I call this savory assembly a "birthday cake," but I've served it at weddings too, and I've never seen an actual cake disappear so fast. Kids especially love being able to reach in and pull a piece of sandwich out of the tantalizing tower.

Time is of the essence; it's best when the sandwiches are still hot. There are a lot of moving parts that make it tricky for one person to get the timing right; enlisting two or even three people will make the process smooth like butter.

You will need three nested springform pans, approximately 6 in [15 cm], 8 in [20 cm], and 10 in [25 cm]; three large baking sheets; and an electric griddle or stove-top griddle pan. If you can find bread you like made in the round loaves called *boules,* they are easier to work with for this recipe—the curves of the bread fit better into the springform pans than rectangular loaves.

1 cup [220 g] salted butter, at room temperature

42 slices rustic artisan bread such as sourdough or levain, preferably cut from 5 to 6 *boules* (see recipe introduction)

21 slices mild, medium, or sharp Cheddar cheese

21 slices Monterey Jack cheese

14 strips thick-sliced bacon, cooked until crisp and drained

2 jalapeño chiles, cut crosswise into slices about ¼ in [6 mm] thick (see Note, page 150)

1 can processed cheese spread with a decorative nozzle, any flavor (optional, but hilarious)

1) Spread the butter on one side of each bread slice, dividing it evenly. Place ten slices, buttered-side down, on a clean cutting board or counter top. Place one slice of Cheddar, one slice of Jack, and another slice of bread, buttered-side up, on top of each. Move the ten plain cheese sandwiches onto one of the baking sheets (it's okay to crowd them).

2) Next, place seven pieces of bread, buttered-side down, on the cutting board. Place one slice of Cheddar, two strips of bacon, one slice of Jack, and another slice of bread, buttered-side up, on top of each. Move the seven bacon-cheese sandwiches onto the second baking sheet.

3) Next, place four pieces of bread, buttered-side down, on the cutting board. Place one slice of Cheddar, three or four rounds of jalapeño, one slice of Jack, and another slice of bread, buttered-side up, on top of each. Move the jalapeño-cheese sandwiches onto the third baking sheet. (At this point, you can wrap the baking sheets tightly with plastic wrap and refrigerate for up to 1 day.)

CONT'D

4) Preheat the oven to 350°F [180°C] and preheat your griddle to medium-high. While the oven is heating, get your workspace ready for assembly. Have a spatula, clean cutting board, and bread knife close by. Remove the bottoms from all of the springform pans. Place a serving platter at least 12 in [30.5 cm] in diameter nearby and place the large springform ring, snapped closed, on top of the serving platter. (Or just assemble on your serving surface.)

5) Place the baking sheet with the plain cheese sandwiches in the oven and bake for 2 to 3 minutes, or until the cheese is beginning to melt. (If the sand-wiches came straight from the refrigerator, it may take another minute or two.) The bread will not be very brown, but don't worry; this step is to get the cheese melting. Remove the baking sheet from the oven, set aside, and put the bacon sandwiches in the oven for 2 to 3 minutes. Meanwhile, move the plain sandwiches to the hot griddle. Watch the sand-wiches on the griddle carefully; they will toast quickly, 30 to 60 seconds on the first side. Turn and brown on the second side, then transfer to a cutting board. The bacon sandwiches should be coming out of the oven right about the time the plain sandwiches are coming off the griddle. When there is space on the griddle, add the bacon sandwiches, and place the jalapeño sandwiches in the oven for 2 to 3 minutes. Continue in this manner until all of the sandwiches have been baked and grilled.

6) Working quickly, fit about four whole hot plain grilled cheeses into the largest springform ring, directly on the serving platter. Cut pieces out of a fifth grilled cheese to fill in any sizeable gaps in the first layer. (If you have helpers, one can tackle this step while someone else toasts the sandwiches on the griddle.) Repeat to make a second layer in the large springform ring with the remaining plain sandwiches. Arrange the second layer so that the seams between individual sandwiches and pieces are offset. This should use up most or all of the ten plain grilled cheeses.

7) Place the medium springform ring, snapped closed, directly on top of the assembled bottom layer, and then repeat this process to fill with the bacon sandwiches. Then place the smallest spring-form ring directly on top of the medium layer and repeat with the jalapeño sandwiches.

8) Unlatch the smallest springform ring to widen it and carefully lift it off the top layer. Then unlatch and remove the middle ring, and finally remove the bottom ring. Tuck in any sandwich pieces that become dislodged. If desired, decorate the cake with the processed cheese spread (florets on each layer are easiest).

9) Serve immediately, but don't cut the cake—tell your guests to pull out the piece they want.

SOUP

Soup is grilled cheese's partner in crime (or lunchtime). Tomato soup and a simple Cheddar grilled cheese is an iconic combination, and our quick, savory Ten-Minute Tomato Soup is optimized for that kind of dipping. In fact, it pairs well with all the grilled cheeses in this book. The soup kitchen on display in this chapter features a number of other puréed soups such as cauliflower, broccoli, potato, celery, and butternut squash that also make great dipping and sipping companions to the sandwiches in this book, plus an assortment of chunky soups to serve on the side.

When pairing soup and grilled cheese, think about complementary flavors and textures. A soup with a bright bite of fresh vegetables, like Broccoli-Cheddar Soup (page 98), Celery Purée Soup (page 102), or Spiced Coconut-Carrot Soup (page 110), will play well with heartier sandwiches such as the American Dip Grilled Cheese (page 85) or Cubano Grilled Cheese (page 72). The richer mixes like Baked Potato Soup (page 100), Pulled Pork Stew (page 115), and American Chili (page 116) will shine when paired with a simpler sandwich such as the Mousetrap Grilled Cheese (page 38) with roasted tomatoes or Mac 'n' Cheese Grilled Cheese (page 42).

TEN-MINUTE TOMATO SOUP

SERVES 6 AS A SIDE DISH

This simple, smooth tomato soup is the result of months of dedicated testing. I wanted the ultimate dipping soup: smooth and savory, with an acidic bite and chile kick to balance out a rich and hearty grilled cheese. I tried dozens of combinations of spices before I hit on the combination of smoky Spanish *pimentón* and the complex, fruity chile from Basque country in France called *piment d'Espelette,* both well known to enhance the flavor of tomatoes.

Strained tomatoes are a very smooth purée, and are key to the texture and simplicity of this soup. We like Pomi and Strianese brands, which can be found in many grocery stores. Top with your favorite croutons to add a little crunch. You can make this soup gluten-free by simply substituting gluten-free flour mix for the all-purpose flour.

3 Tbsp salted butter

2 Tbsp all-purpose flour

1 tsp sugar

½ tsp kosher salt

½ tsp *pimentón* (smoked paprika)

½ tsp *piment d'Espelette* chile powder or cayenne pepper

3¼ cups [780 ml] strained tomatoes

2¼ cups [540 ml] chicken stock

1 tsp balsamic vinegar

Crème fraîche, sour cream, or plain Greek yogurt for garnish

1) In a small soup pot over medium-low heat, melt the butter. When the butter is melted, whisk in the flour, sugar, salt, *pimentón,* and *piment d'Espelette.* Cook, whisking constantly, until the mixture has a nutty, savory aroma, about 3 minutes.

2) Whisk the strained tomatoes, chicken stock, and vinegar into the butter mixture until smooth. Raise the heat to bring to a simmer, stirring occasionally, and simmer gently for about 5 minutes.

3) Ladle the soup into bowls, garnish with a dollop of crème fraiche, and serve immediately.

BROCCOLI-CHEDDAR
SOUP

SERVES 6 AS A SIDE DISH

Broccoli soup has long been recognized as a leading way to get kids (and some adults) to eat broccoli. We've all had prepared brands of this soup, but it can be a revelation when made from scratch at home—the flavors are fresh and bright and you'll never buy canned again. The Cheddar is an accent note rather than the dominating flavor in this version, and the chile powder adds just a little kick. Don't throw away those broccoli stems—peel the tough outer skin, then shred them and toss into Kale Slaw (page 163).

1 Tbsp salted butter

1 medium yellow onion, cut into ½-in [12-mm] dice

1 medium carrot, peeled and cut into ½-in [12-mm] dice

1 garlic clove, minced

1½ lb [680 g] broccoli florets, coarsely chopped

4 cups [960 ml] chicken stock

1 bay leaf

½ tsp minced fresh thyme or ¼ tsp dried thyme

½ tsp *piment d'Espelette* chile powder or cayenne pepper

½ cup [120 ml] heavy cream

1¼ cups [170 g] shredded mild, medium, or sharp Cheddar cheese

Kosher salt and freshly ground black pepper

1) In a small soup pot over medium heat, melt the butter. Add the onion and carrot and cook, stirring often, until the vegetables have softened and the onion is translucent, about 8 minutes. Add the garlic and cook, stirring, for 1 minute longer.

2) Add the broccoli, chicken stock, bay leaf, thyme, and *piment d'Espelette* and stir to combine. Raise the heat to bring to a low boil, then lower the heat to maintain a gentle simmer. Cover and cook, stirring occasionally, until the broccoli is very soft, about 30 minutes. Remove from the heat and discard the bay leaf.

3) Use an immersion blender to blend the soup into a smooth purée in the pot. (If you don't have an immersion blender, purée the soup in a blender, working in batches on low speed. Remove the plug from the lid, cover the lid with a clean towel, and hold down the lid while blending, or the hot soup will blow the lid off and make a mess in the kitchen.) Add the cream and blend for a few seconds more.

4) Return the soup to the stove and reheat gently over low heat. Add the cheese and stir in one direction until the cheese is fully melted into the soup. Season with salt and black pepper.

5) Ladle the soup into bowls and serve immediately.

KALE AND POTATO
SOUP

SERVES 6 AS A SIDE DISH

This soup comes together quickly and is loaded with healthful vegetables. It's hearty enough to be a meal by itself, or makes a great soup-and-salad lunch combination. We use dinosaur kale, so-called because the pebbled dark green leaves look like dinosaur skin, but you can use regular green kale, or even green or red chard, if dinosaur kale is not readily available. The easiest way to remove the ribs and chop the kale is to hold the stem of each leaf in one hand, place the thumb and forefinger of your other hand at the base of the leaf and pull your hand up the rib, stripping the leaf right off the rib. Then stack the stripped leaves neatly, roll together into a tight bundle, and chop the roll into pieces.

1 Tbsp olive oil

1 medium yellow onion, cut into ¼-in [6-mm] dice

2 garlic cloves, minced

About 1 lb [455 g] dinosaur (also called Lacinato or Tuscan) kale, tough stems and ribs removed, leaves coarsely chopped (into about 1-in [2.5-cm] pieces)

3 medium Yukon gold potatoes, peeled and cut into ½-in [12-mm] cubes

1 large ripe tomato, cut into ¼-in [6-mm] dice

4 cups [960 ml] vegetable stock

One 15-oz [425-g] can cannellini beans, drained and rinsed

Kosher salt and freshly ground black pepper

1) In a small soup pot over medium heat, warm the olive oil. Add the onion and cook, stirring often, for about 5 minutes, or until the onion is softened and translucent.

2) Add the garlic and kale and stir for 1 minute to wilt the kale. Add the potatoes, tomato, and vegetable stock and stir to combine. Raise the heat to bring to a low boil, then lower the heat to maintain a gentle simmer. Cover and cook until the potatoes are tender throughout, about 15 minutes. Stir in the beans and simmer for about 10 minutes longer. Season with salt and pepper.

3) Ladle the soup into bowls and serve immediately.

BAKED POTATO
SOUP

SERVES 6 AS A SIDE DISH

This thick and creamy elixir is one of the most popular soups we've created. We call it Baked Potato Soup because the potatoes, chives, and cream make it taste just like a loaded baked potato in soup form. It's a great dunking soup that goes well with all of our sandwiches, but we particularly like it with the American Dip Grilled Cheese (page 85)—the horse-radish cream featured there is also the perfect garnish for this soup. Just spoon a dollop on top of each bowl before serving.

4 cups [960 ml] hot water

1½ lb [680 g] russet potatoes, peeled and cut into ½-in [12-mm] cubes

Kosher salt

2 Tbsp salted butter

1 shallot, minced

1 small leek, trimmed and tough green tops removed, halved lengthwise and carefully washed, cut into ¼-in [6-mm] dice

2 large garlic cloves, minced

2½ cups [600 ml] chicken stock

2 cups [480 ml] whole milk

½ cup [120 ml] heavy cream

Freshly ground black pepper

Chopped crisp-cooked bacon and minced fresh chives for garnish

1) In a small soup pot over medium-high heat, com-bine the water, potatoes, and 1 Tbsp salt and bring to a boil. Lower the heat to maintain a gentle boil and cook, stirring occasionally, until the potatoes are very soft and falling apart, about 15 minutes. Drain the potatoes in a colander, then return them to the pot and set aside.

2) While the potatoes are cooking, heat a medium skillet over medium-low heat. Add 1 Tbsp of the butter, the shallot, and leek and cook, stirring often, until the vegetables have softened, about 6 minutes. Add the garlic and cook, stirring, for 1 minute longer. Remove from the heat and set aside.

3) Return the pot with the potatoes to medium-high heat and add the chicken stock, milk, and cooked vegetables. Bring to a low boil, then lower the heat to maintain a gentle simmer. Cover partially and cook, stirring often, until the potatoes are very mushy, about 20 minutes. Remove from the heat and stir in the heavy cream and remaining 1 Tbsp butter.

4) Use an immersion blender to blend the soup into a smooth purée in the pot. (If you don't have an immersion blender, purée the soup in a blender, working in batches on low speed. Remove the plug from the lid, cover the lid with a clean towel, and hold down the lid while blending, or the hot soup will blow the lid off and make a mess in the kitchen.) Season with salt and pepper.

5) Ladle the soup into bowls, sprinkle with the bacon and chives, and serve immediately.

CELERY PURÉE
SOUP

SERVES 6 AS A SIDE DISH

This creamy soup, redolent of celery and thyme, pairs perfectly with grilled cheese, and is particularly good with the Mushroom-Gruyère Grilled Cheese (page 46). Don't worry that the celery fibers don't fully break down. I like the bit of texture that they add, but if you like your soup perfectly smooth, just press it through a sieve in a few small batches and discard the celery fibers.

3 Tbsp salted butter

1 medium head celery, leafy tops and tough base removed, stalks coarsely chopped

½ lb [230 g] Yukon gold potatoes, peeled and coarsely chopped

1 medium yellow onion, coarsely chopped

1 garlic clove, minced

½ cup [120 ml] dry white wine such as Sauvignon Blanc or Chardonnay

1 tsp minced fresh thyme or ½ tsp dried thyme

4 cups [960 ml] chicken stock

⅓ cup [80 ml] heavy cream

Kosher salt and freshly ground black pepper

1) In a small soup pot over medium-low heat, melt the butter. Add the celery, potatoes, onion, and garlic and cook, stirring often, until the vegetables have softened and are translucent, about 15 minutes.

2) Add the wine and thyme to the vegetables, raise the heat to medium-high, and cook, stirring often, until the wine is reduced by about half, about 5 minutes.

3) Add the chicken stock, cover, and bring to a low boil, then lower the heat to maintain a gentle simmer. Cook until the potatoes are very soft and falling apart, about 20 minutes. Remove from the heat and stir in the cream.

4) Use an immersion blender to blend the soup into a smooth purée in the pot. (If you don't have an immersion blender, purée the soup in a blender, working in batches on low speed. Remove the plug from the lid, cover the lid with a clean towel, and hold down the lid while blending, or the hot soup will blow the lid off and make a mess in the kitchen.) Season with salt and pepper.

5) Ladle the soup into bowls and serve immediately.

LUSCIOUS MUSHROOM
SOUP

SERVES 6 AS A SIDE DISH

Don't even try to compare this elegant concoction to canned cream of mushroom soup. Fresh, homemade, earthy, and herbal—it's a whole different ball game, and a true treat for mushroom lovers. This soup pairs nicely with pretty much every grilled cheese in the book. I like this soup with nice chunks of mushrooms remaining, but you can purée the soup until smooth if you prefer.

2 Tbsp salted butter

1½ tsp olive oil

1 small shallot, minced

1 garlic clove, minced

6 oz [170 g] cremini mushrooms, brushed clean and sliced

5 oz [140 g] shiitake mushrooms, stemmed, brushed clean, and sliced

5 oz [140 g] button mushrooms, brushed clean and sliced

1 Tbsp all-purpose flour

3 cups [720 ml] vegetable stock

3 Tbsp cooking sherry

1 tsp minced fresh thyme or ½ tsp dried thyme

Kosher salt and freshly ground black pepper

3 Tbsp heavy cream

1) In a small soup pot over medium heat, warm the butter with the olive oil until the butter is mostly melted. Add the shallot and sauté until softened, about 3 minutes. Add the garlic and cook for 1 minute longer.

2) Add all of the mushrooms and stir to coat with the fat. Add the flour, vegetable stock, sherry, thyme, 1 tsp salt, and 1 tsp pepper and stir to combine. Raise the heat to bring to a boil, then turn the heat to medium-low, cover, and simmer gently until the mushrooms are very tender, about 15 minutes. Remove from the heat.

3) Use an immersion blender to blend the soup very briefly, just about 5 seconds—you want to thicken the soup but leave lots of nice chunks of mushroom. (If you don't have an immersion blender, blend 1 cup [240 ml] of the soup in a blender on low speed for 5 seconds. Remove the plug from the lid, cover the lid with a clean towel, and hold down the lid while blending, or the hot soup might blow the lid off and make a mess in the kitchen. Return the puréed portion to the pot and stir to combine.) Taste and adjust the seasoning with salt and pepper. Stir in the cream.

4) Ladle the soup into bowls and serve immediately.

FRESH CORN
CHOWDER

SERVES 6 AS A SIDE DISH

This chowder is a popular special during the summer; we often go through fifty ears of just-picked corn a day. The sweet corn shines through the cream and herbs, while the potatoes add body, and a pinch of chile powder adds a little kick to cut through the richness of the cream. Serve this with a salad made with ripe, fresh heirloom tomatoes. To cut kernels from a fresh cob of corn, cut the cob in half crosswise, stand the halves up on the thicker end on a clean cutting board and then carefully run a sharp knife down all sides of the standing cob to cut off the kernels.

1 Tbsp salted butter

1½ tsp olive oil

1 medium yellow onion, cut into ¼-in [6-mm] dice

1 large garlic clove, minced

1 tsp minced fresh thyme or ½ tsp dried thyme

1 Tbsp plus 2 tsp all-purpose flour

3 cups [720 ml] vegetable stock

¾ cup [180 ml] heavy cream

2 medium Yukon gold potatoes, peeled and cut into ¼-in [6-mm] dice

Kernels from 3 ears fresh corn or 2 cups [340 g] frozen corn kernels, drained

¾ tsp *piment d'Espelette* chile powder or cayenne pepper

Kosher salt and freshly ground black pepper

1 Tbsp minced fresh flat-leaf parsley

1) In a medium soup pot over medium heat, melt the butter in the olive oil. Add the onion and cook, stirring often, until translucent, about 8 minutes. Add the garlic and thyme and cook for 1 minute longer.

2) Sprinkle the flour into the onion mixture gradually, whisking constantly to prevent lumps. Stir in the vegetable stock and raise the heat to bring to a low boil. Add the cream and potatoes and return to a boil. Lower the heat to maintain a gentle simmer, cover, and cook, stirring occasionally, until the potatoes can be easily pierced with a fork, about 7 minutes.

3) Stir in the corn and *piment d'Espelette* and season with salt and pepper. Simmer, stirring occasionally, until the corn is tender, about 10 minutes longer. Remove from the heat and stir in the parsley.

4) Ladle the chowder into bowls and serve immediately.

CURRY-CAULIFLOWER
SOUP

SERVES 6 AS A SIDE DISH

I roast the cauliflower before adding it to this soup, which produces a delicious caramelized flavor that is perfectly complemented by the light touch of curry.

1 large head cauliflower, cut into 2-in [5-cm] chunks

1 Tbsp olive oil

Kosher salt and freshly ground black pepper

1 Tbsp salted butter

½ medium yellow onion, diced

1 garlic clove, minced

3 Tbsp all-purpose flour

1 cup [240 ml] whole milk

½ cup [120 ml] heavy cream

2 cups [480 ml] vegetable stock

2 tsp curry powder

¼ tsp cayenne pepper

5 oz [140 g] mild, medium, or sharp Cheddar cheese, shredded, plus more for garnish

Minced fresh chives for garnish (optional)

1) Preheat the oven to 375°F [190°C]. Line a baking sheet with parchment paper or aluminum foil.

2) In a large bowl, combine the cauliflower, olive oil, ½ tsp salt, and ½ tsp black pepper and toss to mix well. Spread the cauliflower in a single layer on the prepared baking sheet and bake until softened and lightly browned, about 20 minutes. Let cool on the pan.

3) In a small soup pot over medium-low heat, melt the butter. Add the onion and sauté until soft and translucent, 5 to 7 minutes. Add the garlic and sauté for 1 minute longer (do not let the garlic burn). Whisk in the flour and cook for 1 minute, stirring constantly. Whisk in the milk, cream, and vegetable stock. Add the roasted cauliflower, curry powder, and cayenne pepper and stir to combine. Raise the heat to bring to a low boil, then turn the heat to low, cover, and simmer until the cauliflower is soft and easily pierced with a fork, about 15 minutes longer. Add the cheese and stir in one direction until the cheese is fully melted into the soup. Remove from the heat.

4) Use an immersion blender to blend the soup into a smooth purée in the pot. (If you don't have an immersion blender, purée the soup in a blender, working in batches on low speed. Remove the plug from the lid, cover the lid with a clean towel, and hold down the lid while blending, or the hot soup will blow the lid off and make a mess in the kitchen.) Taste and adjust the seasoning with salt and black pepper.

5) Ladle the soup into bowls, sprinkle with the chives (if using) and more cheese, and serve immediately.

BUTTERNUT SQUASH
SOUP

SERVES 6 AS A SIDE DISH

I love the silky-smooth texture of this gorgeous, golden butternut squash soup. Pair it with the Thanksgiving Leftovers Grilled Cheese (page 66) for the ultimate post-holiday meal. The sweetness of the butternut squash is perfectly offset by the savory onion and chicken stock. How is this butternut squash soup different from all of the others? We add garam masala, a spice mix from northern India, and coconut milk for a truly distinctive flavor.

One 2-lb [910-g] butternut squash, halved lengthwise, seeds and strings removed

2 tsp olive oil

1 Tbsp salted butter

1 medium yellow onion, cut into ¼-in [6-mm] dice

1 large garlic clove, minced

3 cups [720 ml] chicken stock

1 tsp garam masala

½ tsp minced fresh thyme or ¼ tsp dried thyme

½ tsp minced fresh sage or ¼ tsp dried rubbed sage, crumbled

Pinch of cayenne pepper

Kosher salt and freshly ground black pepper

½ cup [120 ml] Thai-style canned coconut milk or heavy cream

1) Preheat the oven to 375°F [190°C]. Line a baking sheet with parchment paper or aluminum foil.

2) Brush the cut sides of the squash with the olive oil and place both halves, cut-side down, on the prepared baking sheet. Pierce the skin of both halves several times with a fork or sharp knife. Roast until the flesh is soft and easily pierced with a fork and the skin is beginning to brown, about 30 minutes. Let cool until easy to handle, then scrape the flesh of the squash out of the skin and onto a cutting board. Coarsely chop the roasted squash and set aside. Discard the skin.

3) In a medium soup pot over medium-low heat, melt the butter. Add the onion and cook, stirring often, until the onion is translucent, about 8 minutes. Add the garlic and cook, stirring, for 1 minute longer.

4) Add the roasted squash, chicken stock, garam masala, thyme, sage, cayenne pepper, 1 tsp salt, and ½ tsp black pepper and stir to combine. Raise the heat to bring to a low boil, then lower the heat to maintain a gentle simmer. Cover and cook until the squash is very mushy, about 15 minutes. Remove from the heat.

5) Use an immersion blender to blend the soup into a smooth purée in the pot. (If you don't have an immersion blender, purée the soup in a blender, working in batches on low speed. Remove the plug from the lid, cover the lid with a clean towel, and hold down the lid while blending, or the hot soup will blow the lid off and make a mess in the kitchen.) Add the coconut milk and blend for a few seconds more. Return the soup to the stove and reheat gently over low heat, if needed. Taste and adjust the seasoning with salt and black pepper.

6) Ladle the soup into bowls and serve immediately.

SPICED
COCONUT-CARROT
SOUP

SERVES 6 AS A SIDE DISH

This creamy (but cream-free) carrot soup is fragrant with exotic spices. The sweetness of the carrots is balanced by the richness of coconut milk and a bright note of orange juice. This is also a phenomenal soup to dunk a grilled cheese in—it coats the sandwich just right. This beautifully hued soup is particularly delicious with Moroccan Chicken Grilled Cheese (page 58) and The Catch Grilled Cheese (page 55).

2 Tbsp salted butter

1 large yellow onion, cut into ¼-in [6-mm] dice

1½ lb [680 g] carrots, peeled and cut into ½-in [12-mm] cubes

1 large garlic clove, minced

1 Tbsp ground ginger

1 tsp curry powder

1 tsp ground coriander

½ tsp dry mustard powder

4 cups [960 ml] chicken stock

1 cup [240 ml] Thai-style canned coconut milk

½ cup [120 ml] fresh orange juice

Kosher salt and freshly ground black pepper

1) In a medium soup pot over medium heat, melt the butter. Add the onion and carrots and cook, stirring often, until the carrots have softened and the onion is translucent, about 8 minutes.

2) Add the garlic, ginger, curry powder, coriander, and mustard powder and cook, stirring, until aromatic, about 1 minute. Add the chicken stock and coconut milk and stir to combine. Raise the heat to bring to a low boil, then lower the heat to maintain a gentle simmer. Cover and cook until the carrots are very soft and easily pierced with a fork, about 30 minutes. Remove from the heat and stir in the orange juice.

3) Use an immersion blender to blend the soup into a smooth purée in the pot. (If you don't have an immersion blender, purée the soup in a blender, working in batches on low speed. Remove the plug from the lid, cover the lid with a clean towel, and hold down the lid while blending, or the hot soup will blow the lid off and make a mess in the kitchen.) Return the soup to the stove and reheat gently over low heat, if needed. Season with salt and pepper.

4) Ladle the soup into bowls and serve immediately.

SPLIT PEA
SOUP

SERVES 6 AS A SIDE DISH

Sometimes folks just want a vegetable-packed, super-healthful lunch. In my case, I want my lunch to be half a grilled cheese sandwich with a cup of vegetable-packed soup. This soup is easy to make, fresh and delicious, and reheats well. I like to make a batch early in the week and bring it to work for a quick, healthy, no-fuss lunch.

2 tsp olive oil

1 small white onion, cut into ¼-in [6-mm] dice

2 medium carrots, cut into ¼-in [6-mm] dice

2 celery stalks, cut into ¼-in [6-mm] dice

1 large garlic clove, minced

4 cups [960 ml] vegetable stock

⅔ cup [130 g] dried split peas

1 medium Yukon gold potato, peeled and cut into ¼-in [6-mm] dice

1 bay leaf

Kosher salt and freshly ground black pepper

½ tsp ground cumin

¼ tsp ground coriander

1 Tbsp minced fresh flat-leaf parsley

1) In a small soup pot over medium-low heat, warm the olive oil. Add the onion, carrots, and celery and cook, stirring often, until the vegetables have softened, about 8 minutes. Stir in the garlic and cook for 1 minute longer.

2) Add the vegetable stock, split peas, potato, bay leaf, ½ tsp salt, ½ tsp pepper, cumin, and coriander and stir to combine. Raise the heat to bring to a low boil, then lower the heat to maintain a gentle simmer. Cover and cook, stirring occasionally, until the peas are soft, about 30 minutes. Taste and adjust the seasoning with salt and pepper. Stir in the parsley and discard the bay leaf.

3) Ladle the soup into bowls and serve immediately.

SMOKY LENTIL
SOUP

SERVES 6 AS A SIDE DISH

Loaded with healthful vegetables and protein-rich lentils, this chunky easy-to-make soup is hearty enough to make a meal by itself, but we recommend you pair it with a simple sandwich like the Mousetrap Grilled Cheese (page 38). The acidity from the tomato paste and the smoky flavor from the bacon and *pimentón* are great foils for the buttery richness of the sandwich. If you wish to make this soup vegetarian, you can use vegetable stock instead of chicken stock and omit the bacon; the *pimentón* will still supply plenty of smoke.

2 tsp olive oil

1 small white onion, cut into ¼-in [6-mm] dice

2 medium carrots, peeled and cut into ¼-in [6-mm] dice

2 celery stalks, cut into ¼-in [6-mm] dice

2 large garlic cloves, minced

One 6-oz [170-g] can tomato paste

4 cups [960 ml] chicken stock

¾ cup [150 g] green lentils

Kosher salt and freshly ground black pepper

¾ tsp *pimentón* (smoked paprika)

2 strips thick-sliced bacon, cooked until crisp, drained, and coarsely chopped

1) In a small soup pot over medium-low heat, warm the olive oil. Add the onion, carrots, and celery and cook, stirring often, until the vegetables have softened, about 8 minutes. Stir in the garlic and cook for 1 minute longer.

2) Stir in the tomato paste, chicken stock, lentils, 1½ tsp salt, ½ tsp pepper, and the *pimentón*. Raise the heat to bring to a low boil, then lower the heat to maintain a gentle simmer. Cover and cook, stirring occasionally, until the lentils are very tender, about 30 minutes. Remove from the heat and stir in the bacon. Taste and adjust the seasoning with salt and pepper.

3) Ladle the soup into bowls and serve immediately.

WHITE BEAN AND HAM
SOUP

SERVES 6 AS A SIDE DISH

Comforting with smoky ham and nourishing white navy beans, this satisfying soup gets a bright herbal note from rosemary and is great on a cold night. Pair it with a Reubenesque Grilled Cheese (page 89) or a Foghorn Leghorn Grilled Cheese (page 56), or serve it for supper with a simple green salad and a hunk of French bread.

2 Tbsp salted butter

1 medium white onion, cut into ¼-in [6-mm] dice

2 medium carrots, peeled and cut into ¼-in [6-mm] dice

2 celery stalks, cut into ¼-in [6-mm] dice

5 cups [1.2 L] chicken stock

One 15-oz [425-g] can navy beans, drained and rinsed

8 oz [240 g] ham, cut into ¼-in [6-mm] dice

½ tsp minced fresh rosemary or ¼ tsp dried rosemary, crumbled

1 Tbsp minced fresh flat-leaf parsley

Kosher salt and freshly ground black pepper

1) In a small soup pot over medium heat, melt the butter. Add the onion, carrots, and celery and cook, stirring often, until the vegetables have softened and the onion is translucent, about 8 minutes.

2) Add the chicken stock, beans, ham, and rosemary and stir to combine. Bring to a low boil, then turn the heat to low, cover partially, and simmer gently until the beans are heated through and soft but not yet falling apart and the vegetables are very soft, about 20 minutes. Remove from the heat and stir in the parsley. Season with salt and pepper.

3) Ladle the soup into bowls and serve immediately.

PULLED PORK
STEW

SERVES 4 AS A MAIN DISH OR 8 AS A SIDE DISH

I developed this recipe when I realized how much flavor was left in the pan after I made slow-cooked pulled pork. The staff were saving the drippings and smearing them on bread as a snack, and I knew I had to find other delicious uses for the concentrated flavors of this overlooked gift. I added a variety of vegetables to complement the smoky flavors of the pork rub, including leeks, potatoes, mushrooms, and fennel—and just like that, a pretty spectacular stew was born. Serve with a hunk of crusty bread and a simple salad for a complete meal, or pair a smaller portion with a Mousetrap Grilled Cheese (page 38) or the Feta Fetish Grilled Cheese (page 50).

2 Tbsp olive oil

1 medium yellow onion, halved lengthwise through the stem end and cut crosswise into half-moon slices about ¼ in [6 mm] thick

1 small leek, trimmed and tough green tops removed, halved lengthwise and carefully washed, cut crosswise into half-moon slices about ¼ in [6 mm] thick

2 medium Yukon gold potatoes, peeled and cut into ½-in [12-mm] cubes

4 oz [115 g] cremini mushrooms, brushed clean and quartered

2 medium carrots, peeled and cut into ½-in [12-mm] cubes

2 celery stalks, cut into ½-in [12-mm] cubes

1 small fennel bulb, tops and tough core removed, cut into ¼-in [6-mm] dice

1 small ripe tomato, cut into ½-in [12-mm] cubes

1 small shallot, minced

2 garlic cloves, minced

4 cups [960 ml] chicken stock

2 cups [340 g] pulled pork (see page 72), plus ¼ cup [60 ml] reserved drippings

Kosher salt and freshly ground black pepper

1) In a large soup pot over medium heat, warm the olive oil until hot but not smoking. Add the onion and leek and cook, stirring often, until the vegetables have softened and the onion is translucent, about 8 minutes.

2) Add the potatoes, mushrooms, carrots, celery, fennel, tomato, shallot, and garlic and stir to coat in the fat and juices, then add the chicken stock, pork, and pork drippings and stir gently to mix well. Bring to a low boil, then lower the heat to maintain a gentle simmer. Cover and cook, stirring occasionally, until the vegetables are very soft, about 1 hour. Remove from the heat. Season with salt and pepper.

3) Ladle the stew into bowls and serve immediately.

AMERICAN
CHILI

SERVES 8 AS A MAIN DISH

Chili means a lot of different things in a lot of different places. In Texas, it's all meat, no beans. In California, it's several kinds of beans, meat optional. My chili is an adaptation of the California style, with ground beef, lots of sautéed vegetables, and rich gravy redolent of garlic and tomatoes. Traditionally, American chili is fairly spicy, while the cheese, minced onion, and sour cream garnishes help tame the heat. If you like your chili extra spicy, add some extra cayenne or half of a habanero, seeded and minced, with the vegetables. If you prefer it mild, leave out the hot sauce and omit the fresh jalapeños.

Serve this on its own, or try this decadent twist we love: a scoop of chili in a bowl with a scoop of Basic Mac 'n' Cheese (page 120) on top. Or bake the two together and use leftover chili to make Chili Mac (page 141).

1 tsp olive oil, plus 1 Tbsp

1 lb [455 g] ground beef

One 7-oz [199-g] can *chipotles en adobo* (smoked jalapeños canned with tomato sauce)

2 garlic cloves, coarsely chopped

3 Tbsp chili powder

1 Tbsp ancho chile powder

1 Tbsp ground cumin

1 tsp *pimentón* (smoked paprika)

2 fresh jalapeño chiles, seeded and coarsely chopped (see Note, page 150)

2 tsp hot sauce such as Tapatío

2 cups [480 ml] vegetable stock

1 red bell pepper, seeded and cut into ¼-in [6-mm] dice

1 green bell pepper, seeded and cut into ¼-in [6-mm] dice

1 Anaheim chile, seeded and cut into ¼-in [6-mm] dice

1 medium yellow onion, cut into ¼-in [6-mm] dice

1 medium carrot, peeled and cut into ¼-in [6-mm] dice

One 15-oz [425-g] can kidney beans, drained and rinsed

One 15-oz [425-g] can black beans, drained and rinsed

One 15-oz [425-g] can pinto beans, drained and rinsed

One 14½-oz [411-g] can chopped fire-roasted tomatoes, with juice

One 15-oz [425-g] can tomato sauce

2 tsp kosher salt

1 tsp freshly ground black pepper

Shredded Cheddar cheese, minced red onion, and sour cream for garnish

1) In a skillet over medium heat, warm the 1 tsp olive oil. Add the ground beef and cook, stirring with a wooden spoon and breaking up any large chunks of beef, just until nicely browned and no pink spots remain, about 5 minutes. Drain, and discard the fat and pan juices. Set aside.

2) While the beef is cooking, in a blender, combine the *chipotles en adobo*, garlic, chili powder, ancho chile powder, cumin, *pimentón*, jalapeños, hot sauce, and ½ cup [120 ml] of the vegetable stock. Blend on low speed until a smooth purée forms. Set aside.

3) In a large saucepan, warm the 1 Tbsp olive oil over medium heat until hot but not smoking. Add both bell peppers, the Anaheim chile, onion, and carrot and cook, stirring often, until the vegetables have softened and the onion is translucent, about 8 minutes.

4) Add the garlic-chile purée to the pan and stir to combine well. Add all of the beans, cooked ground beef, chopped tomatoes with their juices, tomato sauce, remaining 1½ cups [360 ml] vegetable stock, salt, and black pepper and stir well to combine. Raise the heat to medium-high and bring to a low boil, then turn the heat to medium-low so that the sauce barely bubbles. Cover partially and simmer very gently, stirring occasionally, until the vegetables are very soft, about 30 minutes.

5) Ladle the chili into bowls, garnish with a sprinkle of shredded cheese and red onions and a dollop of sour cream, and serve immediately.

MAC 'N' CHEESE

We love all things involving bread and cheese.
To us mac 'n' cheese is just a deconstructed grilled cheese sandwich. Gooey cheese sauce, chewy noodles, and crunchy bread crumb toppings are just the basics. From there we like to go a little crazy and add in crispy bacon, spicy jalapeños, fragrant herbs, a swirl of green pesto, or chunks of savory ham or chicken and elevate this homely dish from a side act to center stage.

Start with Basic Mac 'n' Cheese (page 120) and then customize it to your own tastes. We heartily encourage you to experiment on your own. And remember to use what's in your kitchen as a catalyst—we top ours using leftover biscuits when we have them, or extra bread if we don't.

Mac 'n' cheese can be assembled a day or two advance and baked before serving, so it's a great option for parties or a fast and hot dinner on busy weeknights.

BASIC MAC 'N' CHEESE

SERVES 6

We started making mac 'n' cheese at the request of some of our regulars, who wanted a change to their warm 'n' cheesy lunch options. Our mac quickly took on a life of its own as our staff and customers alike offered suggestions and ideas for variations in flavor and style, and we now sell tray after tray of our mac and make different kinds every day. Some customers go out of their way to visit us when we have their favorite on the specials board.

This mac 'n' cheese is creamy and crunchy, with a topping made from bread crumbs and melted cheese. Feel free to experiment with the types of cheese, shapes of pasta, and fillings that you stir into the mac before baking to make your own signature mac.

8 oz [230 g] elbow, spiral, or other short pasta of your choice

⅓ cup [40 g] all-purpose flour

¾ tsp dry mustard powder (see Note)

½ tsp garlic powder

½ tsp freshly ground black pepper

⅛ tsp cayenne pepper, or more if you like an extra kick

6 Tbsp [85 g] salted butter, at room temperature

1½ cups [360 ml] whole milk

1 cup [240 ml] heavy cream (see Note)

1 lb [455 g] cheese, shredded, plus 2 oz [55 g] (see Note)

1 thick slice bread, torn into pieces (see Note)

1) Bring a medium saucepan of generously salted water (so it tastes like seawater) to a boil over high heat. Add the pasta and stir immediately. Boil the pasta, stirring occasionally, just until al dente, 8 to 10 minutes or according to the package directions (the pasta should be tender but still chewy, not mushy). Drain the pasta in a colander and set aside.

2) While the pasta is cooking, in a small bowl, whisk together the flour, mustard powder, garlic powder, black pepper, and cayenne pepper and set aside.

3) Put the empty pasta pan (no need to wash it) over medium-low heat and add the butter. When the butter is melted, whisk in the flour mixture. Cook, whisking often, until the mixture is beginning to brown and has a pleasant, nutty aroma, about 1 minute. Watch carefully so it does not burn.

4) Slowly whisk the milk and cream into the butter-flour mixture, combining well. Cook, whisking constantly, until the sauce is heated through and just begins to thicken, about 2 minutes. Remove from the heat.

CONT'D

5) Add the 1 lb [455 g] cheese to the sauce gradually, while stirring constantly in one direction with a wooden spoon or silicone spatula. Stir until the cheese is melted into the sauce, then stir in the cooked pasta. Set aside.

6) Put the torn bread in a food processor and pulse until fine bread crumbs form, or chop finely by hand. In a small bowl, toss the bread crumbs with the remaining 2 oz [55 g] cheese. Set aside.

7) Preheat the oven to 400°F [200°C], with the convection option on, if you have it. Butter an 8-in [20-cm] glass or metal baking dish, or coat with nonstick cooking spray (it will make for much easier cleaning later!).

8) Pour the macaroni and cheese into the prepared dish and sprinkle evenly with the bread crumb mixture. (At this point, you can cover the dish tightly with aluminum foil and refrigerate for up to 2 days.) Bake, uncovered, until the topping is toasted and crunchy and the sauce is bubbling around the edges, about 20 minutes. Let cool for about 10 minutes.

9) Ladle the mac into bowls and serve.

NOTES: You can substitute ½ tsp prepared mustard for the mustard powder (just whisk it in with the milk), and substitute 2½ cups [600 ml] half-and-half for the milk and cream.

You can use many different cheeses and can combine as you like. We suggest Cheddar, plain Jack, garlic and/or herb Jack, fontina, mozzarella, Asiago, provolone, Gruyère, blue cheese, or Comté. If you use a strongly flavored cheese like blue or Gruyère, keep it to less than one-fourth of the total cheese.

For the bread slice, either fresh or stale is fine, and almost any kind is good—sourdough, sandwich loaf, or artisan.

GRUYÈRE, GARLIC, AND WHITE WINE MAC

SERVES 6

This is a deceptively elegant mac 'n' cheese. The garlic and white wine add bite and nuance, and make the dish smell like paradise in a pan. Serve with a simple salad made of butter lettuce and mâche (also known as lamb's lettuce) sprinkled with a bit of vinaigrette, and a cold glass of California Chardonnay alongside.

8 oz [230 g] elbow, spiral, or other short pasta of your choice

⅓ cup [40 g] all-purpose flour

¾ tsp dry mustard powder (see Note, page 122)

½ tsp garlic powder

½ tsp freshly ground black pepper

⅛ tsp cayenne pepper, or more if you like an extra kick

6 Tbsp [85 g] salted butter, at room temperature

2 garlic cloves, minced

¼ cup [60 ml] dry white wine such as Chardonnay or Sauvignon Blanc

1½ cups [360 ml] whole milk

1 cup [240 ml] heavy cream (see Note, page 122)

6 oz [170 g] Gruyère cheese, shredded

8 oz [230 g] mild or medium Cheddar cheese, shredded

4 oz [115 g] fontina cheese, shredded

1 thick slice bread, torn into pieces (see Note, page 122)

1) Bring a medium saucepan of generously salted water (so it tastes like seawater) to a boil over high heat. Add the pasta and stir immediately. Boil the pasta, stirring occasionally, just until al dente, 8 to 10 minutes or according to the package directions (the pasta should be tender but still chewy, not mushy). Drain the pasta in a colander and set aside.

2) While the pasta is cooking, in a small bowl, whisk together the flour, mustard powder, garlic powder, black pepper, and cayenne pepper and set aside.

3) Put the empty pasta pan (no need to wash it) over medium-low heat and add the butter. When the butter is melted, whisk in the minced garlic and the flour mixture. Cook, whisking often, until the mixture is beginning to brown and has a pleasant, nutty aroma, about 1 minute. Watch carefully so it does not burn.

4) Slowly whisk the wine, milk, and cream into the butter-flour mixture, combining well. Cook, whisking constantly, until the sauce is heated through and just begins to thicken, about 2 minutes. Remove from the heat.

5) Add 4 oz [115 g] of the Gruyère, the Cheddar, and the fontina to the sauce gradually, while stirring constantly in one direction with a wooden spoon or silicone spatula. Stir until the cheese is melted into the sauce, then stir in the cooked pasta. Set aside.

6) Put the torn bread in a food processor and pulse until fine bread crumbs form, or chop finely by hand. In a small bowl, toss the bread crumbs with the remaining Gruyère. Set aside.

7) Preheat the oven to 400°F [200°C], with the convection option on, if you have it. Butter an 8-in [20-cm] glass or metal baking dish, or coat with nonstick cooking spray (it will make for much easier cleaning later!).

8) Pour the macaroni and cheese into the prepared dish and sprinkle evenly with the bread crumb mixture. (At this point, you can cover the dish tightly with aluminum foil and refrigerate for up to 2 days.) Bake, uncovered, until the topping is toasted and crunchy and the sauce is bubbling around the edges, about 20 minutes. Let cool for about 10 minutes.

9) Ladle the mac into bowls and serve.

FONTINA, MUSHROOM, AND THYME MAC

SERVES 6

This mac, featuring meaty mushrooms, thyme, and creamy fontina sauce, was inspired by an amazing Neapolitan-style pizza served in a lovely neighborhood trattoria near where we live. Thyme and mushrooms are natural friends, with the light citrus notes of the thyme complementing the earthiness of the mushrooms.

8 oz [230 g] elbow, spiral, or other short pasta of your choice

⅓ cup [40 g] all-purpose flour

¾ tsp dry mustard powder (see Note, page 122)

½ tsp garlic powder

½ tsp freshly ground black pepper

⅛ tsp cayenne pepper, or more if you like an extra kick

2 tsp olive oil

4 oz [115 g] shiitake mushrooms, stemmed, brushed clean, and cut into ¼-in [6-mm] dice

8 oz [230 g] cremini mushrooms, brushed clean and cut into ¼-in [6-mm] dice

6 Tbsp [85 g] salted butter, at room temperature

1½ cups [360 ml] whole milk

1 cup [240 ml] heavy cream (see Note, page 122)

1 tsp minced fresh thyme

8 oz [230 g] Monterey Jack cheese, shredded

8 oz [230 g] fontina cheese, shredded

1 thick slice bread, torn into pieces (see Note, page 122)

2 oz [55 g] Gruyère cheese, shredded

1) Bring a medium saucepan of generously salted water (so it tastes like seawater) to a boil over high heat. Add the pasta and stir immediately. Boil the pasta, stirring occasionally, just until al dente, 8 to 10 minutes or according to the package directions (the pasta should be tender but still chewy, not mushy). Drain the pasta in a colander and set aside.

2) While the pasta is cooking, in a small bowl, whisk together the flour, mustard powder, garlic powder, black pepper, and cayenne pepper and set aside.

3) In a small skillet over medium heat, warm the olive oil, swirling to coat the pan. Add all of the mushrooms and cook, stirring constantly, until the mushrooms have softened, about 2 minutes. Remove from the heat and set aside.

4) Put the empty pasta pan (no need to wash it) over medium-low heat and add the butter. When the butter is melted, whisk in the flour mixture. Cook, whisking often, until the mixture is beginning to brown and has a pleasant, nutty aroma, about 1 minute. Watch carefully so it does not burn.

5) Slowly whisk the milk and cream into the butter-flour mixture, combining well. Cook, whisking constantly, until the sauce is heated through and just begins to thicken, about 2 minutes. Remove from the heat and stir in the sautéed mushrooms and the thyme.

6) Add the Monterey Jack and fontina to the sauce gradually, while stirring constantly in one direction with a wooden spoon or silicone spatula. Stir until the cheese is melted into the sauce, then stir in the cooked pasta. Set aside.

7) Put the torn bread in a food processor and pulse until fine bread crumbs form, or chop finely by hand. In a small bowl, toss the bread crumbs with the Gruyère. Set aside.

8) Preheat the oven to 400°F [200°C], with the convection option on, if you have it. Butter an 8-in [20-cm] glass or metal baking dish, or coat with nonstick cooking spray (it will make for much easier cleaning later!).

9) Pour the macaroni and cheese into the prepared dish and sprinkle evenly with the bread crumb mixture. (At this point, you can cover the dish tightly with aluminum foil and refrigerate for up to 2 days.) Bake, uncovered, until the topping is toasted and crunchy and the sauce is bubbling around the edges, about 20 minutes. Let cool for about 10 minutes.

10) Ladle the mac into bowls and serve.

MOZZARELLA, PESTO, AND TOMATO MAC

SERVES 6

Mozzarella, basil, and tomatoes: these are the Three Musketeers of summer cooking. I combined them here into a gooey mac 'n' cheese with a crunchy topping. Where we live, cherry tomatoes are summer flavor bombs, sweet and juicy, with that special fresh-tomato smell and growing in proliferation in backyards all over town. Use the sweetest, ripest tomatoes you can find for this dish. If you don't have the ingredients or the time available to make our Basil-Lavender Pesto, just substitute store-bought basil pesto. We promise it will still be delicious.

8 oz [230 g] elbow, spiral, or other short pasta of your choice

⅓ cup [40 g] all-purpose flour

¾ tsp dry mustard powder (see Note, page 122)

½ tsp garlic powder

½ tsp freshly ground black pepper

⅛ tsp cayenne pepper, or more if you like an extra kick

6 Tbsp [85 g] salted butter, at room temperature

1½ cups [360 ml] whole milk

1 cup [240 ml] heavy cream (see Note, page 122)

10 oz [280 g] fontina cheese, shredded

8 oz [230 g] mozzarella cheese, preferably fresh, shredded

½ pt [170 g] cherry tomatoes, halved

2 Tbsp Basil-Lavender Pesto (page 159)

1 thick slice bread, torn into pieces (see Note, page 122)

1) Bring a medium saucepan of generously salted water (so it tastes like seawater) to a boil over high heat. Add the pasta and stir immediately. Boil the pasta, stirring occasionally, just until al dente, 8 to 10 minutes or according to the package directions (the pasta should be tender but still chewy, not mushy). Drain the pasta in a colander and set aside.

2) While the pasta is cooking, in a small bowl, whisk together the flour, mustard powder, garlic powder, black pepper, and cayenne pepper and set aside.

3) Put the empty pasta pan (no need to wash it) over medium-low heat and add the butter. When the butter is melted, whisk in the flour mixture. Cook, whisking often, until the mixture is beginning to brown and has a pleasant, nutty aroma, about 1 minute. Watch carefully so it does not burn.

4) Slowly whisk the milk and cream into the butter-flour mixture, combining well. Cook, whisking constantly, until the sauce is heated through and just begins to thicken, about 2 minutes. Remove from the heat.

5) Add 8 oz [230 g] of the fontina and the mozzarella to the sauce gradually, while stirring constantly in one direction with a wooden spoon or silicone spatula. Stir until the cheese is melted into the sauce, then stir in the cooked pasta, tomatoes, and pesto. Set aside.

6) Put the torn bread in a food processor and pulse until fine bread crumbs form, or chop finely by hand. In a small bowl, toss the bread crumbs with the remaining fontina. Set aside.

7) Preheat the oven to 400°F [200°C], with the convection option on, if you have it. Butter an 8-in [20-cm] glass or metal baking dish, or coat with nonstick cooking spray (it will make for much easier cleaning later!).

8) Pour the macaroni and cheese into the prepared dish and sprinkle evenly with the bread crumb mixture. (At this point, you can cover the dish tightly with aluminum foil and refrigerate for up to 2 days.) Bake, uncovered, until the topping is toasted and crunchy and the sauce is bubbling around the edges, about 20 minutes. Let cool for about 10 minutes.

9) Ladle the mac into bowls and serve.

CRAB MAC

SERVES 6

A man in a business suit once threw a temper tantrum in the middle of our restaurant when the customer in front of him got the last serving of our Crab Mac. The lemon zest, fresh garlic, and parsley add a bit of zing that brings out the sweetness of the briny crab meat—and the passion of our patrons.

8 oz [230 g] elbow, spiral, or other short pasta of your choice

⅓ cup [40 g] all-purpose flour

¾ tsp dry mustard powder (see Note, page 122)

½ tsp garlic powder

½ tsp freshly ground black pepper

⅛ tsp cayenne pepper, or more if you like an extra kick

6 Tbsp [85 g] salted butter, at room temperature

1½ cups [360 ml] whole milk

1 cup [240 ml] heavy cream (see Note, page 122)

10 oz [280 g] fontina cheese

4 oz [115 g] mild, medium, or sharp Cheddar cheese, shredded

4 oz [115 g] Havarti cheese, shredded

1 lb [455 g] cooked lump crabmeat, fresh or canned, picked over for shell fragments and cartilage

1 Tbsp minced fresh flat-leaf parsley

1 garlic clove, minced

1 tsp grated lemon zest

1 thick slice bread, torn into pieces (see Note, page 122)

1) Bring a medium saucepan of generously salted water (so it tastes like seawater) to a boil over high heat. Add the pasta and stir immediately. Boil the pasta, stirring occasionally, just until al dente, 8 to 10 minutes or according to the package directions (the pasta should be tender but still chewy, not mushy). Drain the pasta in a colander and set aside.

2) While the pasta is cooking, in a small bowl, whisk together the flour, mustard powder, garlic powder, black pepper, and cayenne pepper and set aside.

3) Put the empty pasta pan (no need to wash it) over medium-low heat and add the butter. When the butter is melted, whisk in the flour mixture. Cook, whisking often, until the mixture is beginning to brown and has a pleasant, nutty aroma, about 1 minute. Watch carefully so it does not burn.

4) Slowly whisk the milk and cream into the butter-flour mixture, combining well. Cook, whisking constantly, until the sauce is heated through and just begins to thicken, about 2 minutes. Remove from the heat.

5) Add 8 oz [230 g] of the fontina, the Cheddar, and Havarti to the sauce gradually, while stirring constantly in one direction with a wooden spoon or silicone spatula. Stir until the cheese is melted into the sauce, then stir in the cooked pasta, crabmeat, parsley, minced garlic, and lemon zest. Set aside.

6) Put the torn bread in a food processor and pulse until fine bread crumbs form, or chop finely by hand. In a small bowl, toss the bread crumbs with the remaining fontina. Set aside.

7) Preheat the oven to 400°F [200°C], with the convection option on, if you have it. Butter an 8-in [20-cm] glass or metal baking dish, or coat with nonstick cooking spray (it will make for much easier cleaning later!).

8) Pour the macaroni and cheese into the prepared dish and sprinkle evenly with the bread crumb mixture. (At this point, you can cover the dish tightly with aluminum foil and refrigerate for up to 2 days.) Bake, uncovered, until the topping is toasted and crunchy and the sauce is bubbling around the edges, about 20 minutes. Let cool for about 10 minutes.

9) Ladle the mac into bowls and serve.

BBQ CHICKEN MAC

SERVES 6

This is a great way to use up leftover chicken (fried, roasted, or grilled—it doesn't matter). If you love BBQ chicken pizza, you'll love this mac, too. If you don't have BBQ potato chips on hand, you can use the bread crumb topping we specify in the other mac 'n' cheese recipes.

8 oz [230 g] elbow, spiral, or other short pasta of your choice

⅓ cup [40 g] all-purpose flour

¾ tsp dry mustard powder (see Note, page 122)

½ tsp garlic powder

½ tsp freshly ground black pepper

⅛ tsp cayenne pepper, or more if you like an extra kick

10 oz [280 g] cooked chicken, hand-pulled or chopped into ½-in [12-mm] pieces

⅓ cup [80 ml] barbecue sauce (use your favorite)

6 Tbsp [85 g] salted butter, at room temperature

1½ cups [360 ml] whole milk

1 cup [240 ml] heavy cream (see Note, page 122)

10 oz [280 g] mild, medium, or sharp Cheddar cheese, shredded

8 oz [230 g] Monterey Jack cheese, shredded

1 cup [60 g] barbecue-flavor potato chips

1) Bring a medium saucepan of generously salted water (so it tastes like seawater) to a boil over high heat. Add the pasta and stir immediately. Boil the pasta, stirring occasionally, just until al dente, 8 to 10 minutes or according to the package directions (the pasta should be tender but still chewy, not mushy). Drain the pasta in a colander and set aside.

2) While the pasta is cooking, in a small bowl, whisk together the flour, mustard powder, garlic powder, black pepper, and cayenne pepper and set aside. In a medium bowl, toss the chicken with the barbecue sauce and set aside.

3) Put the empty pasta pan (no need to wash it) over medium-low heat and add the butter. When the butter is melted, whisk in the flour mixture. Cook, whisking often, until the mixture is beginning to brown and has a pleasant, nutty aroma, about 1 minute. Watch carefully so it does not burn.

4) Slowly whisk the milk and cream into the butter-flour mixture, combining well. Cook, whisking constantly, until the sauce is heated through and just begins to thicken, about 2 minutes. Remove from the heat.

5) Add 8 oz [230 g] of the Cheddar and the Monterey Jack to the sauce gradually, while stirring constantly in one direction with a wooden spoon or silicone spatula. Stir until the cheese is melted into the sauce, then stir in the cooked pasta and chicken. Set aside.

6) Place the potato chips in a large zip-top bag. Push all of the air out of the bag and seal it. Slowly roll a rolling pin over the bag until all of the chips are crushed to about the size of coarse bread crumbs. Add the remaining Cheddar to the bag and shake to combine. Set aside.

7) Preheat the oven to 400°F [200°C], with the convection option on, if you have it. Butter an 8-in [20-cm] glass or metal baking dish, or coat with nonstick cooking spray (it will make for much easier cleaning later!).

8) Pour the macaroni and cheese into the prepared dish and sprinkle evenly with the potato chip mixture. (At this point, you can cover the dish tightly with aluminum foil and refrigerate for up to 2 days.) Bake, uncovered, until the topping is brown and crunchy and the sauce is bubbling around the edges, about 20 minutes. Let cool for about 10 minutes.

9) Ladle the mac into bowls and serve.

HAM AND HERB MAC

SERVES 6

Sweet and salty, everyday sandwich lunch meat and also a special holiday celebration feast—what is it about ham? Sure, it takes almost any dish from being a starter or side to a main course, but our macs with ham are always the fastest to sell out; the combo of ham and cheese *and* noodles seems to be a collective dream, evoking childhood holiday fantasies. You can use any kind of ham here, but *jambon de Paris* (cooked French-style ham), Black Forest ham, and honey-baked ham are our favorites for this dish.

8 oz [230 g] elbow, spiral, or other short pasta of your choice

⅓ cup [40 g] all-purpose flour

¾ tsp dry mustard powder (see Note, page 122)

½ tsp garlic powder

½ tsp freshly ground black pepper

⅛ tsp cayenne pepper, or more if you like an extra kick

6 Tbsp [85 g] salted butter, at room temperature

1½ cups [360 ml] whole milk

1 cup [240 ml] heavy cream (see Note, page 122)

6 oz [170 g] Gruyère cheese, shredded

8 oz [230 g] mild, medium or sharp Cheddar cheese, shredded

4 oz [115 g] fontina cheese, shredded

6 oz [170 g] ham, diced

1 tsp minced fresh flat-leaf parsley

1 tsp minced fresh thyme

1 tsp minced fresh rosemary

1 thick slice bread, torn into pieces (see Note, page 122)

1) Bring a medium saucepan of generously salted water (so it tastes like seawater) to a boil over high heat. Add the pasta and stir immediately. Boil the pasta, stirring occasionally, just until al dente, 8 to 10 minutes or according to the package directions (the pasta should be tender but still chewy, not mushy). Drain the pasta in a colander and set aside.

2) While the pasta is cooking, in a small bowl, whisk together the flour, mustard powder, garlic powder, black pepper, and cayenne pepper and set aside.

3) Put the empty pasta pan (no need to wash it) over medium-low heat and add the butter. When the butter is melted, whisk in the flour mixture. Cook, whisking often, until the mixture is beginning to brown and has a pleasant, nutty aroma, about 1 minute. Watch carefully so it does not burn.

4) Slowly whisk the milk and cream into the butter-flour mixture, combining well. Cook, whisking constantly, until the sauce is heated through and just begins to thicken, about 2 minutes. Remove from the heat.

5) Add 4 oz [115 g] of the Gruyère, the Cheddar, and fontina to the sauce gradually, while stirring constantly in one direction with a wooden spoon or silicone spatula. Stir until the cheese is melted into the sauce, then stir in the cooked pasta, ham, parsley, thyme, and rosemary. Set aside.

6) Put the torn bread in a food processor and pulse until fine bread crumbs form, or chop finely by hand. In a small bowl, toss the bread crumbs with the remaining Gruyère. Set aside.

7) Preheat the oven to 400°F [200°C], with the convection option on, if you have it. Butter an 8-in [20-cm] glass or metal baking dish, or coat with nonstick cooking spray (it will make for much easier cleaning later!).

8) Pour the macaroni and cheese into the prepared dish and sprinkle evenly with the bread crumb mixture. (At this point, you can cover the dish tightly with aluminum foil and refrigerate for up to 2 days.) Bake, uncovered, until the topping is toasted and crunchy and the sauce is bubbling around the edges, about 20 minutes. Let cool for about 10 minutes.

9) Ladle the mac into bowls and serve.

ASIAGO, PROSCIUTTO, AND SAGE MAC

SERVES 6

Choose a young Asiago (Asiago Pressato), which will bring a sweeter, nuttier flavor to this Italian-inflected dish than you will get with an aged Asiago. The salty prosciutto and earthy sage round out this delicious and sophisticated mac.

8 oz [230 g] elbow, spiral, or other short pasta of your choice

⅓ cup [40 g] all-purpose flour

¾ tsp dry mustard powder (see Note, page 122)

½ tsp garlic powder

½ tsp freshly ground black pepper

⅛ tsp cayenne pepper, or more if you like an extra kick

6 Tbsp [85 g] salted butter, at room temperature

1½ cups [360 ml] whole milk

1 cup [240 ml] heavy cream (see Note, page 122)

10 oz [280 g] Asiago cheese, shredded

8 oz [230 g] fontina cheese, shredded

3 oz [85 g] thinly sliced prosciutto, chopped into ¼-in [6-mm] pieces

1 tsp minced fresh sage or ½ tsp dried rubbed sage

1 thick slice bread, torn into pieces (see Note, page 122)

1) Bring a medium saucepan of generously salted water (so it tastes like seawater) to a boil over high heat. Add the pasta and stir immediately. Boil the pasta, stirring occasionally, just until al dente, 8 to 10 minutes or according to the package directions (the pasta should be tender but still chewy, not mushy). Drain the pasta in a colander and set aside.

2) While the pasta is cooking, in a small bowl, whisk together the flour, mustard powder, garlic powder, black pepper, and cayenne pepper and set aside.

3) Put the empty pasta pan (no need to wash it) over medium-low heat and add the butter. When the butter is melted, whisk in the flour mixture. Cook, whisking often, until the mixture is beginning to brown and has a pleasant, nutty aroma, about 1 minute. Watch carefully so it does not burn.

4) Slowly whisk the milk and cream into the butter-flour mixture, combining well. Cook, whisking constantly, until the sauce is heated through and just begins to thicken, about 2 minutes. Remove from the heat.

5) Add 8 oz [230 g] of the Asiago and the fontina to the sauce gradually, while stirring constantly in one direction with a wooden spoon or silicone spatula. Stir until the cheese is melted into the sauce, then stir in the cooked pasta, prosciutto, and sage. Set aside.

6) Put the torn bread in a food processor and pulse until fine bread crumbs form, or chop finely by hand. In a small bowl, toss the bread crumbs with the remaining Asiago. Set aside.

7) Preheat the oven to 400°F [200°C], with the convection option on, if you have it. Butter an 8-in [20-cm] glass or metal baking dish, or coat with nonstick cooking spray (it will make for much easier cleaning later!).

8) Pour the macaroni and cheese into the prepared dish and sprinkle evenly with the bread crumb mixture. (At this point, you can cover the dish tightly with aluminum foil and refrigerate for up to 2 days.) Bake, uncovered, until the topping is toasted and crunchy and the sauce is bubbling around the edges, about 20 minutes. Let cool for about 10 minutes.

9) Ladle the mac into bowls and serve.

BACON AND JALAPEÑO MAC

SERVES 6

We added mac 'n' cheese to the menu at the behest of our customers, but we started having fun with it right away, just like we did, and do, with our grilled cheese sandwiches. This was our first, and is still one of our best, variations. On a whim, I added a few handfuls of chopped cooked bacon and fresh diced jalapeños to this mix, and was entranced by the results. I think the staff ate the whole first tray; the customers had to wait until the next day, when we eagerly made this magnificent, fire-and-smoke mac again.

8 oz [230 g] elbow, spiral, or other short pasta of your choice

⅓ cup [40 g] all-purpose flour

¾ tsp dry mustard powder (see Note, page 122)

½ tsp garlic powder

½ tsp freshly ground black pepper

⅛ tsp cayenne pepper, or more if you like an extra kick

6 Tbsp [85 g] salted butter, at room temperature

1½ cups [360 ml] whole milk

1 cup [240 ml] heavy cream (see Note, page 122)

10 oz [280 g] mild, medium or sharp Cheddar cheese, shredded

4 oz [115 g] fontina cheese, shredded

4 oz [115 g] Monterey Jack cheese, shredded

4 or 5 strips thick-sliced bacon, cooked until crisp, drained, and chopped

1 jalapeño chile, seeds and ribs removed, cut into ¼-in [6-mm] dice (see Note, page 150)

1 thick slice bread, torn into pieces (see Note, page 122)

1) Bring a medium saucepan of generously salted water (so it tastes like seawater) to a boil over high heat. Add the pasta and stir immediately. Boil the pasta, stirring occasionally, just until al dente, 8 to 10 minutes or according to the package directions (the pasta should be tender but still chewy, not mushy). Drain the pasta in a colander and set aside.

2) While the pasta is cooking, in a small bowl, whisk together the flour, mustard powder, garlic powder, black pepper, and cayenne pepper and set aside.

3) Put the empty pasta pan (no need to wash it) over medium-low heat and add the butter. When the butter is melted, whisk in the flour mixture. Cook, whisking often, until the mixture is beginning to brown and has a pleasant, nutty aroma, about 1 minute. Watch carefully so it does not burn.

CONT'D

4) Slowly whisk the milk and cream into the butter-flour mixture, combining well. Cook, whisking constantly, until the sauce is heated through and just begins to thicken, about 2 minutes. Remove from the heat.

5) Add 8 oz [230 g] of the Cheddar, the fontina, and Jack to the sauce gradually, while stirring constantly in one direction with a wooden spoon or silicone spatula. Stir until the cheese is melted into the sauce, then stir in the cooked pasta, bacon, and jalapeño. Set aside.

6) Put the torn bread in a food processor and pulse until fine bread crumbs form, or chop finely by hand. In a small bowl, toss the bread crumbs with the remaining Cheddar. Set aside.

7) Preheat the oven to 400°F [200°C], with the convection option on, if you have it. Butter an 8-in [20-cm] glass or metal baking dish, or coat with nonstick cooking spray (it will make for much easier cleaning later!).

8) Pour the macaroni and cheese into the prepared dish and sprinkle evenly with the bread crumb mixture. (At this point, you can cover the dish tightly with aluminum foil and refrigerate for up to 2 days.) Bake, uncovered, until the topping is toasted and crunchy and the sauce is bubbling around the edges, about 20 minutes. Let cool for about 10 minutes.

9) Ladle the mac into bowls and serve.

CHILI MAC

SERVES 6

Chili on the bottom and mac 'n' cheese on top—what's not to love? This is the perfect use for leftover American Chili, and a great dish to bring to a potluck; everyone loves the chili surprise on the bottom. If you want to make it extra spicy, stir a minced fresh jalapeño into the mac 'n' cheese along with the pasta.

4 oz [115 g] elbow, spiral, or other short pasta of your choice

2½ Tbsp all-purpose flour

½ tsp dry mustard powder (see Note, page 122)

¼ tsp garlic powder

¼ tsp freshly ground black pepper

⅛ tsp cayenne pepper, or more if you like an extra kick

3 Tbsp salted butter, at room temperature

¾ cup [180 ml] whole milk

½ cup [120 ml] heavy cream (see Note)

6 oz [170 g] mild, medium, or sharp Cheddar cheese, shredded

4 oz [115 g] Monterey Jack cheese, shredded

1 thick slice bread, torn into pieces (see Note, page 122)

3 cups [855 g] American Chili (page 116), heated (see Note)

1) Bring a medium saucepan of generously salted water (so it tastes like seawater) to a boil over high heat. Add the pasta and stir immediately. Boil the pasta, stirring occasionally, just until al dente, 8 to 10 minutes or according to the package directions (the pasta should be tender but still chewy, not mushy). Drain the pasta in a colander and set aside.

2) While the pasta is cooking, in a small bowl, whisk together the flour, mustard powder, garlic powder, black pepper, and cayenne pepper and set aside.

3) Put the empty pasta pan (no need to wash it) over medium-low heat and add the butter. When the butter is melted, whisk in the flour mixture. Cook, whisking often, until the mixture is beginning to brown and has a pleasant, nutty aroma, about 30 seconds. Watch carefully so it does not burn.

4) Slowly whisk the milk and cream into the butter-flour mixture, combining well. Cook, whisking constantly, until the sauce is heated through and just begins to thicken, about 2 minutes. Remove from the heat.

CONT'D

5) Add 4 oz [115 g] of the Cheddar and the Jack to the sauce gradually, while stirring constantly in one direction with a wooden spoon or silicone spatula. Stir until the cheese is melted into the sauce, then stir in the cooked pasta. Set aside.

6) Put the torn bread in a food processor and pulse until fine bread crumbs form, or chop finely by hand. In a small bowl, toss the bread crumbs with the remaining Cheddar. Set aside.

7) Preheat the oven to 400°F [200°C], with the convection option on, if you have it. Butter an 8-in [20-cm] glass or metal baking dish, or coat with nonstick cooking spray (it will make for much easier cleaning later!).

8) Pour the chili into the prepared dish and spread evenly. Carefully spoon the mac 'n' cheese over the chili and sprinkle evenly with the bread crumb mixture. (At this point, you can cover the dish tightly with aluminum foil and refrigerate for up to 2 days.) Bake, uncovered, until the topping is toasted and crunchy and the sauce is bubbling around the edges, about 20 minutes. Let cool for about 10 minutes.

9) Ladle the mac into bowls and serve.

NOTES: You can substitute 1¼ cups [300 ml] half-and-half for the milk and cream.

If you are baking right away, gently rewarm the chili in a small saucepan over medium-low heat until hot, or microwave it in a heatproof bowl for about 2 minutes, or until warmed through, before topping with the mac 'n' cheese. If you are making the mac ahead of time and will be refrigerating before cooking, then cold chili is preferable.

PICKLES, SPREADS, AND SIDES

If the blank grilled cheese sandwich is a canvas waiting to be painted and the primary colors are the bread and the cheese, then these pickles and spreads will give you a great set of bright accent colors to play with. Tart magenta Pickled Red Onions (page 151), sweet-hot deep orange Apricot-Jalapeño Relish (page 155), and bright green Basil-Lavender Pesto (page 159) add scintillating flashes of color—but, more important, they add a spectrum of flavors to balance out the rich, melted cheese. The assertive flavors in these toppings and spreads provide contrast and texture that can turn even an everyday grilled cheese into something truly special.

I've included a couple of my favorite side dishes here: our Kale Slaw (page 163), a simple salad packed with fresh veggies and laced with Greek yogurt dressing; and the super-savory Muffaletta Olive Salad (page 157), which adds richness to any light bite. All the recipes in this chapter provide fun, light, and fresh complements to a toasty, hot, melty grilled cheese.

BREAD 'N' BUTTER PICKLES

MAKES ABOUT 1 QT [455 G]

We go through about three hundred cucumbers a week to make these addictive Bread 'n' Butter Pickles, putting them on a variety of sandwiches and selling them by the jar in our shops. Once you realize how easy it is to make your own pickles (not to mention how much tastier they are), you'll never buy supermarket pickles again.

1 lb [455 g] pickling cucumbers, scrubbed and cut into ¼-in- [6-mm-] thick rounds

1 Tbsp prepared horseradish, not cream-style

1 Tbsp dried dill

1 cup [240 ml] white vinegar

1 cup [200 g] sugar

4 garlic cloves, peeled

2 Tbsp pickling spice

1 Tbsp ground turmeric

1 Tbsp kosher salt

1 tsp black peppercorns

1) Pack the cucumber rounds into a 1-qt [960-ml] glass canning jar with a secure lid. Add the horseradish and dill, screw on the lid, and shake gently to distribute.

2) In a small saucepan over high heat, combine the vinegar, sugar, garlic, pickling spice, turmeric, salt, and peppercorns and stir thoroughly. Bring to boil and immediately remove from the heat.

3) Open the jar and pour the hot brine over the cucumbers. Add cold water to fill the container, leaving ¼-in [6-mm] headspace, and stir gently. Let cool at room temperature for 20 minutes, then replace the lid tightly and gently shake the jar to ensure the pickles are covered in the brine and the horseradish and dill are evenly dispersed.

4) Refrigerate for 6 hours before serving. Consume within 4 weeks.

GIARDINIERA

MAKES ABOUT 3 CUPS [675 G]

Giardiniera (pronounced "jar-din-YARE-uh") is an Italian American condiment made with a variety of different vegetables, a mixture of herbs, and sometimes vinegar. Rain Hayes, a good friend and multitalented cook extraordinaire, developed this recipe after traveling to Chicago and falling instantly in love with this very sexy condiment. She gave me the original recipe that inspired the Windy City Grilled Cheese (page 84), and now we use only this version in our sandwiches.

When hot peppers are added to giardiniera, it's sometimes called "hot mix." We add hot jalapeño and habanero chiles to ours, so if you're struggling to pronounce *giardiniera*, you have an easy alternative. For our rendition, we dice the vegetables quite small, to make it easier to portion and spread in a grilled cheese. As with many of the recipes in this book, I encourage you to experiment—try zucchini, gherkins, or different kinds of olives.

1 green bell pepper, cut into ¼-in [6-mm] dice

1 red bell pepper, cut into ¼-in [6-mm] dice

1 jalapeño chile, seeded and minced (see Note)

1 habanero chile, seeded and minced (see Note; optional)

1 medium carrot, peeled and cut into ¼-in [6-mm] dice

1 celery stalk, cut into ¼-in [6-mm] dice

½ cup [60 g] cauliflower florets, cut into ¼-in [6-mm] dice

½ medium white onion, cut into ¼-in [6-mm] dice

Kosher salt

1 garlic clove, minced

1½ tsp dried oregano

½ tsp red pepper flakes

Freshly ground black pepper

½ cup [120 ml] white vinegar

¼ cup [60 ml] olive oil

¼ cup [60 ml] grapeseed or canola oil

2½ oz [70 g] pimiento-stuffed green olives, drained and finely chopped

1) In a large glass or plastic bowl, combine both bell peppers, the jalapeño, habanero (if using), carrot, celery, cauliflower, onion, and ¼ cup [75 g] salt and toss to mix. Add enough cold water just to cover the vegetables. Cover tightly with plastic wrap and refrigerate for 8 to 12 hours.

2) Drain the vegetables in a colander set in the sink, reserving the bowl. Rinse the vegetables under cold running water and set aside.

CONT'D

3) In a small bowl, whisk together the garlic, oregano, red pepper flakes, ¼ tsp black pepper, and the vinegar. Slowly but thoroughly whisk in the olive oil and grapeseed oil, forming an emulsion. Stir in the green olives.

4) Put the drained vegetables back in the reserved bowl. Pour the oil-vinegar mixture over the vegetables and toss together with a spoon to combine well and coat thoroughly. Season with salt and pepper if needed, and then pack into nonreactive glass jars or plastic storage containers and cover tightly.

5) Refrigerate for 24 hours before serving. Consume within 4 weeks.

NOTE: To prepare hot chiles, wear gloves or use a fork and knife, or the chile seeds will burn your fingers—and any other part of your body you touch (like your eyes!)—after handling them. Cut the top off the chile and slice the body in half vertically. Then, using a gloved finger or a fork and knife, carefully scrape out the ribs and seeds and discard before slicing or chopping the chile as directed. Much of the fire is in those seeds, so add a few back in if you like it hot. And be aware that the heat of chiles can vary widely. I always eat a tiny piece of the chile in question before adding it to any dish so that I can adjust the amount I use to my own, or my diners', taste.

PICKLED RED ONIONS

MAKES ABOUT 2 CUPS [450 G]

A classic condiment in Mexican cuisine, these quick and easy—and pretty—pickled onions can be added to salads, roasted pork, or chicken dishes, or serve with a cheese board and crackers for a colorful flourish.

¾ cup [180 ml] white vinegar

1 Tbsp sugar

1 small cinnamon stick

3 whole cloves

1 bay leaf

1 whole star anise

¼ tsp red pepper flakes

1 medium red onion, thinly sliced

1) In a small saucepan over medium heat, stir together the vinegar, sugar, cinnamon stick, cloves, bay leaf, star anise, and red pepper flakes. Bring to a boil, then remove from the heat. Cover the pan and let the spices steep for 5 minutes.

2) Add the onion slices to the saucepan and stir well. Pour the mixture into a 1-qt [960-ml] glass jar or plastic storage container and cover tightly.

3) Refrigerate for 4 hours before serving. Consume within 4 weeks.

SWEET PICKLED JALAPEÑOS

──────●────────

MAKES ABOUT 1½ CUPS [340 G]

Hot and sweet at the same time, these pickled jalapeño rings are a delicious addition to the Mousetrap Grilled Cheese (page 38) and Mac 'n' Cheese Grilled Cheese (page 42), are fantastic on burgers, and just bring general excitement to almost any appetizer, cheese board, or sandwich bar.

½ cup [120 ml] hot water (the hottest water from your tap is fine)

2 Tbsp apple cider vinegar

⅓ cup [80 ml] white vinegar

1½ tsp honey

1 tsp black peppercorns

1 garlic clove, chopped

1 Tbsp kosher salt

1 bay leaf

4 oz [115 g] fresh jalapeño peppers, cut into rings about ¼ in [6 mm] thick (see Note, page 150)

1) In a small saucepan over medium heat, stir together the hot water, cider vinegar, white vinegar, honey, peppercorns, garlic, salt, and bay leaf. Bring to a boil, then remove from the heat. Cover the pan and let the spices steep for 5 minutes.

2) Add the jalapeños to the saucepan and stir well. Pour the mixture into a 1-pt [480-ml] glass jar or plastic storage container and cover tightly.

3) Refrigerate for 1 day before serving. Consume within 4 weeks.

PRESERVED MEYER LEMONS

MAKES 1 QT [740 G]

Originally from China and thought to be a cross between a "true" lemon and a Mandarin orange, Meyer lemons have a thin, sweet, and floral rind and pulp that is less acidic than regular lemons yet still intensely lemony. They make terrific cocktails and desserts, but preserving them in salt intensifies their flavors and softens the edible rinds. Preserved or pickled lemons are a traditional flavor in northern African and southern Asian cuisine. You can buy preserved Meyer lemons at specialty shops, but if you can find fresh Meyer lemons in season and are willing to plan ahead, you can have a jar of this delicious condiment in your refrigerator year-round.

Preserved lemons and grilled cheese may seem like a strange combination, but we use these floral, salty-sweet flavor bombs in a variety of ways in our restaurant, adding them to sandwich spreads, fried chicken brine, even soup.

8 Meyer lemons, thoroughly cleaned and patted dry, cut lengthwise into quarters

Kosher salt

1) Pack a layer of lemon quarters in the bottom of a clean 1-qt [960-ml] glass canning jar with a secure lid. Sprinkle about 1 Tbsp kosher salt on top. Repeat, alternating layers of lemon and salt, until the jar is loosely full. Push the lemons down into the jar so their juice is released and cram as many more lemon quarters as you can into the jar—the goal is to get the air out and the lemons and salt in.

2) When you've packed the jar as full as you can, sprinkle an extra layer of salt on top and seal the jar tightly with the lid.

3) Refrigerate for 4 weeks before serving. Consume within 6 months.

CRANBERRY SAUCE

Fresh cranberry sauce is so ridiculously fast and easy to make, there's really no reason to buy it in cans. It's also surprisingly adaptable; you can add warm spices, as we do, or stir in orange zest for a bright, tangy cranberry sauce. Homemade cranberry sauce is one of my favorite guilty pleasures; I'll eat it with a spoon right out of the container. Its tangy sweetness is a great addition to any turkey or chicken sandwich, and I also love spooning it over vanilla ice cream for a quick dessert.

3 cups [340 g] fresh or frozen whole cranberries
¾ cup [180 ml] cold water
1 cup [200 g] sugar
Pinch of ground cinnamon
Pinch of ground cloves

1) In a medium saucepan, combine the cranberries, water, sugar, cinnamon, and cloves. Bring to a boil over medium heat, stirring to help dissolve the sugar. Turn the heat to medium-low and simmer, stirring often, until most of the berries have popped and the sauce has thickened slightly, about 5 minutes.

2) Remove from the heat and let cool to room temperature before serving. Store in an airtight container in the refrigerator for up to 1 month.

APRICOT-JALAPEÑO RELISH

MAKES ABOUT 2½ CUPS [455 G]

Everyone loves this relish so much in our Jalapeño Popper Grilled Cheese (page 68) and Breakfast Popper Grilled Cheese (page 25), we started selling it by the jar in our shops. The chunky texture and sweet-hot flavor is just right for burgers, roast pork loin, or grilled chicken. Make an easy canapé by topping crackers with a dollop of chèvre and a spoonful of relish. To make it extra spicy, add a finely chopped habanero chile to the mix (see Note, page 150).

4 medium jalapeño chiles, seeded and cut into ¼-in [6-mm] dice

2 small serrano chiles, seeded and cut into ¼-in [6-mm] dice

½ small white onion, cut into ¼-in [6-mm] dice

2 cups [240 g] dried apricots, cut into ¼-in [6-mm] dice

1½ Tbsp apple cider vinegar

1 Tbsp fresh lime juice

1 Tbsp peeled and grated fresh ginger, or 1 tsp ground ginger

2 tsp kosher salt

1½ tsp dry mustard powder

1) In a medium glass or plastic bowl, combine all the chiles, the onion, apricots, vinegar, lime juice, ginger, salt, and mustard powder and stir to mix thoroughly. Pack the relish into glass canning jars or plastic storage containers and cover tightly.

2) Refrigerate overnight to allow the flavors to blend before serving. Consume within 3 weeks.

KALAMATA TAPENADE

MAKES ABOUT 1 CUP [170 G]

In addition to using this super-savory tapenade in grilled cheeses, it's delicious spread on toasted crostini, tossed into pasta dishes, or layered with greens, tomatoes, and feta for a quick, rich and tangy Mediterranean salad.

1 cup [140 g] pitted Kalamata olives, drained

1 Tbsp balsamic vinegar

3 garlic cloves

1½ tsp capers, drained

¾ cup [20 g] loosely packed fresh flat-leaf parsley leaves, minced

1) In a food processor, combine the olives, vinegar, garlic, and capers and pulse in 3-second increments until finely chopped, scraping down the sides of the bowl as needed. Scrape the mixture into a small bowl and fold in the parsley by hand. (If you don't have a food processor, mince the olives, garlic, and capers by hand and toss them with the vinegar and parsley in a small bowl.) Pack the tapenade into glass canning jars or plastic containers and cover tightly.

2) Store in the refrigerator for up to 2 weeks or in the freezer for up to 4 weeks (thaw gently in the refrigerator or at room temperature before using).

MUFFALETTA OLIVE SALAD

MAKES ABOUT 1 CUP [230 G]

It's called a "salad," but this is really somewhere between a tapenade and sandwich spread—we have no idea why the gods of sandwiches past decided to call it Olive Salad. The primary use of olive salad is in muffaletta sandwiches, and you can enjoy this recipe in our Muffaletta Grilled Cheese (page 81). However, if you have some extra, you can also make an easy and tasty side salad by tossing a spoonful of it with hand-torn butter lettuce and halved cherry tomatoes.

½ cup [75 g] pimiento-stuffed green olives, drained and finely chopped

½ cup [75 g] pitted Greek black olives, drained and finely chopped

¼ cup [35 g] finely chopped roasted red peppers

2 canned roasted artichoke hearts, drained

½ shallot, minced

2 Tbsp minced fresh flat-leaf parsley

1 Tbsp fresh lemon juice

1 garlic clove, minced

½ tsp capers, drained and finely chopped

½ teaspoon dried oregano

1) In a medium bowl, combine the green olives, black olives, red peppers, artichoke hearts, shallot, parsley, lemon juice, garlic, capers, and oregano. Toss to mix well and transfer to an airtight container.

2) Refrigerate for 8 hours before serving. Consume within 4 weeks.

MOROCCAN GREEN OLIVE, ARTICHOKE, AND PRESERVED LEMON SPREAD

MAKES ABOUT 1 CUP [230 G]

Sure, this salty-tangy-meaty spread is great on grilled cheese, but it is also excellent spooned onto toasted bruschetta or tossed with tuna, cucumbers, and tomatoes and served over mixed greens for a tasty salad. To enlist it for an easy main course, brush boneless, skinless chicken breasts with a bit of olive oil; sprinkle with salt and pepper; and coat thickly with the olive-artichoke spread. Bake in a 350°F [180°C] oven until cooked through and the juices run clear, about 20 minutes.

We use bright-green Castelvetrano olives from southern Italy in our spread, both for the flavor and the color. These olives are processed in lye rather than being cured, and the flavor is sweeter and fruitier than black or cured olives. The bright green olives, yellow lemon, and fresh herbs make for an eye-catching spread.

½ cup [70 g] pitted green Castelvetrano olives

½ cup [70 g] drained jarred artichoke hearts

2 garlic cloves, chopped

2 Tbsp Preserved Meyer Lemons (page 153), seeds removed and coarsely chopped

1 Tbsp minced fresh cilantro

1 Tbsp minced fresh flat-leaf parsley

In a food processor or blender, combine the olives, artichoke hearts, garlic, and preserved lemon. Pulse until a uniformly textured, slightly chunky spread forms. Using a rubber spatula, scrape the spread into a small bowl and fold in the cilantro and parsley. Store in an airtight container in the refrigerator for up to 1 month.

BASIL-LAVENDER PESTO

MAKES ABOUT ⅓ CUP [75 G]

The cheese makes any grilled cheese sandwich rich enough, so I left out the traditional nuts and cheese in this dedicated pesto recipe. As a result, the concentrated herbal flavor really stands out. Substitute a handful or so of arugula, spinach, or parsley for half of the basil to add a different herbal note, if you wish.

2 cups [60 g] packed fresh basil leaves, thick stems removed

1 tsp food-grade dried lavender buds

1½ Tbsp olive oil

1 tsp kosher salt

½ tsp freshly ground black pepper

In a food processor or blender, combine the basil, lavender buds, olive oil, salt, and pepper. Process, stopping to scrape down the sides with a rubber spatula two or three times, until a uniformly textured, easily spreadable paste forms, about 2 minutes. Use immediately; or transfer to a small bowl, place plastic wrap directly on the pesto to prevent browning, and refrigerate for up to 5 days; or freeze in a small airtight container for up to 1 month.

APPLE MUSTARD

MAKES ABOUT 1 CUP [240 G]

I came up with this recipe after pondering an important question: What are our favorite things to combine with Cheddar cheese? Apples and mustard topped the list, so I started there. A delicious place to start—but I found that adding sweet, rich caramelized onions really made this spread special. It's sweet, salty, and savory all at the same time. If you have extra, serve it with roast pork loin or pork chops, or just spread it on toast and enjoy.

1 Tbsp vegetable oil

1 medium yellow onion, cut into ¼-in [6-mm] dice

½ tsp kosher salt

⅓ cup [80 g] stone-ground mustard

⅓ cup [80 g] apple butter (see Sources, page 168)

1) In a small skillet over medium heat, warm the vegetable oil. Add the onion and salt and stir to combine. Cover and cook, stirring every couple of minutes, until the onion is translucent and soft, about 8 minutes. Uncover, raise the heat to medium-high, and cook, stirring often to prevent scorching, until the onion is the color of light brown sugar, about 8 minutes longer. Remove from the heat and let cool for about 10 minutes.

2) Combine the mustard, apple butter, and caramelized onion in a food processor or blender and process until smooth, stopping to scrape down the sides at least once. Use immediately, or store in an airtight container in the refrigerator for up to 2 weeks.

NOTE: If you have leftover caramelized onions, try spreading 1 Tbsp inside the bread of a Mousetrap Grilled Cheese (page 38) or a Mushroom-Gruyère Grilled Cheese (page 46) before cooking.

BALSAMIC ONION MARMALADE

MAKES ABOUT 1½ CUPS [340 G]

If you haven't had onion marmalade, you're in for a treat. Sweet and piquant, it's a perfect complement in our Roast Beef and Blue Cheese Grilled Cheese (page 83), but it is equally delightful in a simple grilled cheese with mild Cheddar and a few crumbles of your favorite blue cheese, or just on a cracker with a sliver of good cheese.

2 tsp vegetable oil

2 medium red onions, cut into ¼-in [6-mm] dice

1 tsp kosher salt

½ tsp freshly ground black pepper

¼ cup [50 g] sugar

¼ cup plus 2 Tbsp [85 ml] balsamic vinegar

1) In a small saucepan over medium heat, warm the vegetable oil. Add the onions, salt, and pepper and stir to combine. Cook, stirring every couple of minutes, until the onions are soft and translucent, about 8 minutes.

2) Stir in the sugar and continue to cook, stirring occasionally, until the liquid from the onions and melted sugar is reduced but the mixture is not yet sticking to the pot, about 8 minutes longer. Turn the heat to medium-low, stir in the vinegar, and cook, stirring often to prevent scorching, until the liquid is reduced to a thick syrup and the mixture is starting to stick to the pan, about 30 minutes.

3) Remove from the heat and let cool to room temperature. Store in an airtight container in the refrigerator for up to 2 weeks.

KALE SLAW

SERVES 4

After joyously making thousands of grilled cheese sandwiches, even we have come to recognize an inalienable truth: Man cannot live on grilled cheese alone. It's always great to add a refreshing crunchy salad packed with vegetables. This easy kale slaw can be as varied as what you find in your refrigerator—carrots, Brussels sprouts, broccoli stems (trim the toughest part, but the rest is delicious!), asparagus, apples, onions, radicchio, peas. Shred all the veggies you use thoroughly and more or less evenly for the most pleasing texture.

DRESSING
½ cup [110 g] plain Greek yogurt (regular or low fat)

⅓ cup [85 g] mayonnaise

2 Tbsp fresh lemon juice

2 Tbsp apple cider vinegar

1 Tbsp sugar

1 Tbsp celery seeds

½ tsp kosher salt

½ tsp freshly ground black pepper

SLAW
½ bunch dinosaur (Lacinato) kale, stems removed

¼ head green cabbage, tough core removed

½ red bell pepper, seeded

4 oz [115 g] jicama, peeled

¼ fennel bulb, fronds and tough dark green part removed

¼ cup [45 g] dried currants

1) To make the dressing: In a medium bowl, whisk together the yogurt, mayonnaise, lemon juice, vinegar, sugar, celery seeds. salt, and pepper until smooth. Set aside.

2) To make the slaw: In a food processor fitted with the 2-mm slicing blade (4 mm is also okay, but the 2-mm is slightly better), slice the kale, cabbage, and bell pepper. Transfer the sliced vegetables to a large bowl. Replace the slicing blade with the shredding blade, shred the jicama and fennel and add them to the kale mix. (If your food processor is too small, work in batches, adding one or two vegetables at a time and transferring them to a large bowl as you finish.) Add the currants to the bowl and toss together to mix thoroughly.

3) Drizzle the dressing over the slaw (you may not need all of it), toss to coat lightly, and serve immediately.

GLOSSARY

BREADS

9-grain/multigrain: There is no set list of grains that go into multigrain bread, but some of the common ones include whole wheat, rye, triticale, barley, oats, buckwheat, spelt, emmer, millet, and flax. These are hearty breads with nutty flavors and rough textures from the grains.

Brioche: Soft, slightly sweet, and chewy white yeast bread enriched with eggs and butter; similar to challah, but sweeter.

Challah: Similar to brioche but usually less sweet; traditionally formed into a braided loaf and eaten on Jewish holidays.

Ciabatta: The Italian name translates as "slipper," and this bread is shaped as such—a long, fairly flat white yeasted loaf. Its characteristic large holes form during the rise and baking. The texture is very chewy and the flavor is mild, similar to Italian bread.

Focaccia: Light, flat, yeasted Italian bread, generally baked in a large sheet 1 to 2 in [2.5 to 5 cm] thick and often deeply dimpled on the surface with the fingertips of the baker before it goes into the oven to ensure an even rise. Focaccia may be brushed with olive oil and rosemary or other herbs before baking.

Italian loaf: A mild white bread with a soft interior and crunchy crust, formed into a large oblong loaf.

Miche: A rustic French sourdough with a high percentage of whole-wheat flour, usually made with natural sourdough culture and shaped into a very large round loaf.

Oat: Oat bread is made with a combination of oats and wheat flour, and has a dense, moist texture. It is usually baked as a sandwich loaf and sold sliced. It may be sweetened with honey.

Naan: A leavened white or whole-wheat flatbread baked at high temperatures. Popular in India and throughout South and Central Asia. Can be flavored with garlic or onions, or stuffed with potatoes or other fillings, but the flavor is usually somewhat plain and the texture fairly soft.

Pain au levain: Made from French-style wild-yeast sourdough starter (the "levain") and often some whole-wheat and some white flour; shaped as a *batard*. Levain is chewy, with a well-developed structure, and the flavor is somewhat like a mild sourdough with some nuttiness from the whole wheat.

Pain de campagne: French country-style loaf shaped in a large round. Usually made with some whole wheat, this bread is chewy and hearty.

Pain de mie: Slightly sweet and dense white French sandwich loaf.

Pretzel rolls/pretzel bread: While pretzels are traditionally shaped into knots, pretzel dough, which is a mild, yeasted white bread treated with lye or soda to give it the characteristic pretzel flavor and dark brown glossy finish, may be baked into rolls or even a loaf.

Pumpernickel: Heavy, dense, slightly sweet, dark pure rye often made with mixed flour, whole-grain berries, and molasses.

Rye: A dense and dark bread made since the middle ages with varying proportions of rye flour mixed with wheat flour. Rye has a somewhat stronger flavor than wheat bread.

Semolina: Semolina is a finely ground high-gluten flour made from the hard, coarse endosperm of durum wheat. Bread made from semolina has a light golden color and fine moist texture.

Sourdough: California sourdough is a white bread made with wild yeasts that result in a sour flavor. It may be shaped in a sandwich loaf, round, or *batard*.

Whole-wheat: Also called whole-grain or wholemeal bread, whole-wheat bread is made with some portion (up to 100 percent) milled whole wheat. It is often formed into a sandwich loaf, but may be baked into other shapes, and may have honey added for sweetness. This bread has a moist, dense texture and a wheaty/nutty flavor.

CHEESES

Asiago: An Italian cow's-milk cheese from the Veneto region that can have a variety of textures depending on aging. Younger, softer Asiagos are best for grilled cheeses.

Barely Buzzed Cheddar: A cow's-milk cheese produced by the Beehive Cheese Co. in Utah. This Cheddar is rubbed with lavender and coffee grounds.

Bel Paese: Means "beautiful country" in Italian. A young Italian cow's-milk cheese, pale and creamy with a light buttery flavor.

Blue/bleu: Can be made from cow's milk, sheep's milk, or goat's milk and is produced all over the world. Blue cheese has cultures of *Penicillium* mold added so that the resulting cheese is spotted or veined with blue, blue-gray, or blue-green mold. Blue cheese has a strong, distinctive smell and is often aged in temperature-controlled caves.

Boschetto al Tartufo: A fresh, semisoft Italian cheese made from a combination of cow's and sheep's milk. It is infused with shavings of black truffles.

Brick: A semisoft cow's-milk cheese originating in Wisconsin, brick cheese gets its name from the brick shapes the cheeses are formed in. Similar to Cheddar, but with a softer texture and sharper finish.

Brie: A soft, mild, creamy cow's-milk cheese with a pale color and a rind of white mold. The rind is typically eaten.

Butterkäse: The name translates to "butter cheese" from German, and is a good description of this cheese. It is a very mild, buttery semisoft cow's-milk cheese popular in Germany and commonly sold as a loaf for easy slicing.

Cantal: One of the oldest cheeses made in France, this is a semihard to hard cow's-milk cheese aged 1 to more than 6 months. Flavors are similar to Cheddar, tangy and buttery.

Carmody: A semisoft cow's-milk cheese made in California by Bellwether Farms. Young and buttery, with fresh milk flavors, this cheese was named after a road running alongside the dairy.

Cheddar: Hard cow's-milk cheese originating in the English village of Cheddar and made since at least the twelfth century, this cheese is now made into dozens of styles in regions all over the world. Color ranges from white to dark yellow and flavor is buttery and sharp.

Cheshire: A dense semihard cow's-milk cheese made in Cheshire county, England. Has a moist, crumbly texture and mild, salty taste.

Chèvre: Fresh goat's-milk cheese that can be crumbled or spread. This tangy and creamy cheese is made all over the world, but particularly in France and California.

Colby: A semihard fresh cow's-milk cheese named for the town of Colby, Wisconsin, where it originated, this mild cheese is similar to Cheddar but is softer in texture and has more moisture. Often combined with Jack cheese and sold as Colby Jack, which can be substituted.

Comté: Also called *Gruyère de Comté,* a semihard yellow unpasteurized French cow's-milk cheese aged 8 to 12 months. One of the most popular cheeses in France, it has a nutty, caramelized flavor.

Crescenza: Also called *Stracchino*, this soft, creamy Italian cow's-milk cheese is usually formed into squares. It is eaten very young and has a mild and delicate flavor.

Double Gloucester: A semihard cow's-milk cheese made in Gloucestershire, England, since the sixteenth century. Aged for 4 months.

Edam: Also called *Edammer,* this semihard cheese made from cow's or goat's milk originated in the Netherlands. It is usually formed into balls and covered in red wax, and has a mild, slightly salty and nutty flavor and a lower fat content than most cheeses.

Emmenthaler: Also called *Emmental*, a Swiss cow's-milk cheese that is medium to hard in texture with large holes (called eyes). It has a flavor reminiscent of mass-market Swiss cheese but more complex and subtle, caused by bacteria introduced during the cheesemaking process.

Fontina: A semisoft cow's-milk cheese originating from Italy's Aosta Valley and now also made in Denmark, France, Canada, and the United States. Traditional Italian Fontina Val d'Aosta is an unpasteurized pungent cheese with a natural rind, but most other versions are much milder, with a wax rind, and may be pasteurized.

Gorgonzola: A soft, crumbly, veined Italian blue cheese made from unskimmed cow's milk that can be somewhat salty. It was named after the town of Gorgonzola that it originates from, and has been made for centuries.

Gouda: A semihard Dutch cow's-milk cheese named after the town of origin, but now made in several countries around the world. This cheese can be young or aged and flavors and textures can vary widely. Young Gouda is typically very mild and creamy, but aged Gouda has nutty, butterscotch flavors with an almost sweet finish. This is one of the oldest recorded cheeses in the world, dating back to the twelfth century! Gouda may be smoked or flavored with the addition of fenugreek, cumin, or other herbs and spices.

Gruyère: Named for the town of Gruyères in Switzerland where it originated, this yellow semihard or hard cow's-milk cheese is aged for 5 to 12 months. It is now also made in the United States. The flavor varies depending on age, but is generally sweet and slightly salty, with a distinct earthy aroma.

Havarti: Also called cream Havarti or creamy Havarti, this is a Danish semisoft cow's-milk cheese. This is a simple, cream-colored and creamy table cheese, typically with sweet notes, and can be found with a variety of flavorings added, such as dill, cranberry, horseradish, garlic, caraway, and jalapeño.

Ibérico: A hard Spanish cheese made from a mixture of cow's, sheep's, and goat's milk. Flavors are buttery, nutty, and sharp, and the texture may be crumbly.

Idiazábal: A semihard to hard cheese made from unpasteurized sheep's milk from Basque Country in Spain. This cheese is always aged, but the texture and flavor may vary depending on how long. Idiazábal can be smoked after aging, contributing a nutty, buttery, smoky flavor.

Jack, Monterey or Sonoma Jack: An American semisoft cow's-milk cheese, aged 1 to 6 months, pale yellow to white in color and mild in flavor. Melts beautifully and is often flavored with ingredients ranging from garlic to herbs to chiles.

Jarlsberg: A yellow semisoft Norwegian cow's-milk cheese aged for a minimum of 1 year, with a wax rind and large eyes. This is a mild, creamy, versatile cheese with flavors similar to mild Swiss cheese, caused by the addition of bacteria during the cheesemaking process.

Mahón: A creamy, buttery, semisoft Spanish cow's-milk cheese.

Manchego: A hard Spanish sheep's-milk cheese, aged between 2 months and 2 years with a distinctive hard brown rind and somewhat crumbly texture. The flavor is distinctive as well, tasting of the sheep's milk it was made from.

Mimolette: A hard, French cow's-milk cheese with a distinct bright orange interior caused by the addition of annatto coloring, aged two months to two years, and formed into round balls. The flavor when young is mild, and a distinct hazelnut taste emerges in the more aged versions.

Mozzarella: Fresh cheese made from cow's or water buffalo's milk (*mozzarella di bufala*), originating in Italy but now made around the world. This versatile cheese can have varying textures, may be smoked (*scamorza*) or sold packed in oil and herbs, and has very mild flavors that taste of fresh milk.

Muenster: A semisoft cow's-milk cheese. Versions from the United States have a characteristic orange rind and a soft, white, creamy interior. Muenster has a very mild flavor.

Ossau-Iraty: A semihard sheep's-milk cheese from the French Basque region.

Parmesan: *see* Parmigiano-Reggiano

Parmigiano-Reggiano: A hard, unpasteurized, brined and aged cow's-milk cheese originating in Italy. Not a great melting cheese; usually grated to facilitate melting. Pale yellow in color, this cheese is salty with rich umami flavors.

Pecorino: Semihard or hard sheep's-milk cheese made in several regions of Italy; the flavor and texture vary depending on how long it is aged. When young, it is mild and easily sliced or shaved, with flavors of cream and milk, but when aged it is crumbly, nutty, and buttery. In southern Italy, peppercorns or red pepper flakes are added to make *pecorino pepato*.

Port Salut: A semisoft pasteurized cow's-milk cheese from France with mild flavors but a fairly strong smell.

Provolone: A semihard Italian cow's-milk cheese now produced around the world. Typically shaped into a cylinder, young provolone is very mild and slightly salty, while aged provolone may be sharp and pungent.

P'tit Basque: A semihard sheep's-milk cheese from the French Basque region. Pale yellow with a natural rind that looks like Manchego, this mild cheese has grassy and buttery flavors.

Queso Oaxaca: White, semihard cow's-milk cheese from Mexico with mild flavors like Monterey Jack but a stringy texture like mozzarella.

Raclette: This semihard, fairly sharp-tasting French cow's-milk cheese is traditionally served melted in thin slices on top of potatoes, toast, and other ingredients using a special melting tool also called a *raclette*.

Roncal: A hard but creamy Basque sheep's-milk cheese with a fresh herbaceous flavor from Spain's Roncal Valley. Formed into a barrel shape, this cheese has a hard, natural moldy rind.

Sage Derby: A semihard cow's-milk cheese from England that is mottled green and has a subtle herbal flavor created by adding sage to the cheesemaking process.

San Joaquin Gold: A hard cow's-milk cheese, similar to Cheddar, from a dairy in California's San Joaquin Valley. It has a thin natural rind, a pale yellow color, and a mild flavor, with notes of nuts and butter.

Scamorza: Often marketed as smoked mozzarella, Scamorza is a young Italian cow's-milk cheese that is made in a manner similar to mozzarella, but then dried and smoked. It has a white, mild interior and a brown rind from the smoking process.

Swiss: Another name for Emmenthaler; usually called "Swiss cheese" in the United States.

Teleme: An American semisoft cow's-milk cheese originating from the San Francisco Bay Area.

Toma: A cow's-milk cheese from the Point Reyes Farmstead Cheese Company in Northern California. This semihard, mild white cheese is pasteurized and has a natural rind. Flavors are creamy and buttery with a grassy tang finish.

Triple crème: This cow's-milk cheese has at least 75 percent butterfat content, with a texture and natural white moldy rind similar to Brie. Soft and easily spreadable, this cheese will melt quickly, so handle gently.

Urgelia: Also called *Queso de l'Alt Urgell y la Cerdanya*, this is a semisoft cow's-milk cheese from the Catalonia region of northern Spain. This cheese is washed in brine and aged for only 45 days. It has an assertive buttery flavor and melts well.

OTHER

Capicola: Also called *cappicola, capicolla,* and *coppa.* An Italian dry-cured pork *salume* made from a muscle running from the head to the neck of a pig. Similar to prosciutto and often seasoned with white wine, garlic, and various herbs and spices before curing.

Chipotle: A smoked jalapeño. *Chipotle en adobo* is a smoked jalapeño that has been preserved, usually by canning, in a spicy sauce.

Crème fraîche: Cultured cream with a rich mouthfeel and very mild buttermilk flavor. Crème fraîche is similar to mild Greek yogurt or sour cream, and you can substitute those for any recipe calling for crème fraîche.

Garam masala: Translates to "hot spice mix," with "hot" referring to the intensity of the spices, not the capsicum content. This traditional blend from northern India varies regionally but typically includes turmeric, peppercorns, cloves, cinnamon, cumin, and cardamom.

Hass avocado: Smaller, dark-green avocados with rough, pebbled skin. The flavor and texture of Hass avocados is superior to the larger smooth-skinned varieties. You'll know these are ripe when the fruit gives slightly when squeezed gently.

Jambon de Paris: A lean, whole-muscle ham that is delicately spiced and slowly cooked in its own juices. It is always boneless and usually served thinly sliced.

Jamón Serrano: Aged (6 to 18 months), dry-cured ham from the town of Serrano in Spain. Traditionally served sliced very thinly off the bone and served cold. You can also use the more expensive *Jamón Ibérico*, a similar style of ham cured for 2 to 3 years.

Mortadella: A large Italian ground pork sausage from Bologna flavored with spices and pistachios.

Piment d'espelette: Espelette peppers are grown in the Basque region of France. Prized for their nuanced fruity flavors, these mildly hot peppers are usually sold powdered or in a paste. The flavor is unique, but hot paprika can be substituted, if needed.

Pimentón: Smoked Spanish paprika, sold in mild (*dulce*), moderately hot (*agridulce*), or hot (*picante*) versions.

Prosciutto: Italian dry-cured ham usually served thinly sliced, cold, and uncooked. Aged for about 18 months.

Ras el hanout: Translates to "top [or head] of the shop," implying that this Moroccan spice mix is the best the merchant has to offer. The traditional recipe has varying ingredients depending on the source, but typically includes turmeric, peppers, saffron, mace, cinnamon, coriander, cloves, and cardamom.

Speck: An Old English word meaning "fat" or "blubber," also the name for several different pork products across Europe. In this book, "speck" refers to Italian speck, a dry-cured ham similar to prosciutto.

SOURCES

Amazon: Pomi Strained Tomatoes, King Island Dairy's Roaring Forties Blue from Australia and New Zealand. www.amazon.com

B&R Farms: Dried California Blenheim apricots. www.brfarms.com

Beehive Cheese Co: Barely Buzzed Cheddar. www.beehivecheese.com

Bellwether Farms: Carmody cheese. www.bellwetherfarms.com

Blue Chair Fruit: Early Girl Tomato Jam. shop.bluechairfruit.com

Dean & Deluca: *Pimentón*, mace, herbes de Provence, garam masala. www.deandeluca.com

Earth & Vine Provisions: Red Bell Pepper and Ancho Chili Jam, Pumpkin-Orange Marmalade. www.earthnvine.com

Fiscalini: San Joaquin Gold cheese. www.fiscalinicheese.com

Holland's Family Cheese LLC: Marieke Gouda Foenegreek. www.hollandsfamilycheese.com

iGourmet: Wide variety of specialty cheeses. www.igourmet.com

Kozlowski Farms: Apple butter. www.kozlowskifarms.com

McQuade's Celtic Chutneys: Fig 'n' Ginger Chutney. www.mcquadechutneys.com

Point Reyes Farmstead Cheese Company: Toma, Point Reyes Original Blue. www.pointreyescheese.com

San Francisco Herb Co: Pickling spice, dried lavender buds, mace, herbes de Provence, other spices and herbs. www.sfherb.com

Sierra Nevada: Sierra Nevada Stout & Stoneground Mustard. www.sierranevadagiftshop.com

The Spanish Table: Ras el hanout, *pimentón,* preserved meyer lemons. www.spanishtable.com

Williams-Sonoma: Ras el hanout, garam masala, preserved lemons. www.williams-sonoma.com

ACKNOWLEDGMENTS

It takes a village to write a grilled cheese cookbook, and we could not have done this without the help of dozens of friends, family, and professionals—and many of the latter are now friends, too. We had a stroke of luck in opening our first American Grilled Cheese Kitchen less than a block from Chronicle Books, and the Chronicle staff promptly became some of our favorite regulars. They encouraged us to consider writing a cookbook and referred us to the resources we needed to pull it off.

Amanda Poulsen Dix saved our bacon more than once by keeping us organized and on schedule, and led us through the wilderness of writing recipes for public consumption. We could not have done this without you!

Copious thanks to the kind, patient, and wise folks at Chronicle Books who showed us the ropes of cookbook writing. Special shout-out to our editor, Amy Treadwell, and to Peter Perez for his enthusiasm and encouragement over the last several years. Doug Ogan, Carrie Bradley Neves, Vanessa Dina, Tera Killip, Steve Kim . . . thank you all.

We also want to thank the dedicated and talented staff at The American Grilled Cheese Kitchen, many of whom helped develop these recipes. In particular, Adam Maxwell, our kitchen manager, contributed recipes, techniques, and support of all kinds, and Joe Steinocher helped us make all the recipes for the photo shoot. Travis, Elvis, Nikki, Summer, Junior, Georgy, Victor, Melanie, Joey, Rachel, and Will all contributed recipes or ideas that landed in this book in one way or another. Ben Auerbach helped by chopping mounds of *mirepoix*, washing piles of dishes, and gamely eating every sample put in front of him; thank you, David and Suzanne, for donating Ben, and Junior, to the cause!

And of course big thanks to our parents, who encouraged us to leave our office jobs and pursue this crazy dream of grilled cheese in the first place. Jeanne Ormsby, both CFO and CMO (Chief Mom Officer) of The Kitchen, we both owe you so much for your eternal support and guidance. Naomi and Ray Pollak, thank you for your unshakable confidence in and love of us; your perpetual encouragement to "keep on truckin'" motivates us daily. As emigrants from South Africa, you paved your unique way to "make it" in America, inspiring us to do it our way—with lots of grilled cheese. Ray, we doubt any other highly skilled transplant surgeon has cleaned and diced, by hand, more than five hundred pounds of Brussels sprouts. You should be proud.

And thanks to Heidi's late father, Larry Gibson, who never had the chance to visit The American Grilled Cheese Kitchen but who surely would have been its greatest fan and biggest cheerleader. Unbeknownst to him, Larry also gave us the awesome American Chili recipe, one of his specialties from Heidi's childhood. Hopefully his one-pan brownies, thin pancakes, and famous Catalina Eggs will make it into future publications; it would have amused the hell out of him to see his recipes in print.

To those on the ground who have supported us and continue to support us in everything we do, we thank you for perpetually being there. You've made sandwiches, painted walls, fixed pipes, cleaned restaurants, "tweeted," "liked," listened, and loved. And for the purposes of this cookbook, we thank you again for patiently trying yet another grilled cheese or another bowl of soup: Scout Addis (our very first customer!), Terry Sandin, Tackett Austin, Rain Hayes, Marian Reynov, Philippa Manley, Sam Serpente, Ray Tang, Dan Perkel, Roxanne Miller, Ruth Grayson, David Cramer, Joel Pollak, Beth Pollak, Claire Silverman, Mike Gubman, Emily Rolph, Andrew Headington, Laura Headington, Gabe Turow, Liz Seibert, and everyone else who found room for one more taste.

Lastly, props to our dedicated cleanup crew, Stella (we miss you so much!), Mickey, and Tilly, who kept the floors spotless while we cooked.

INDEX

A

American Chili, 116–17
American Dip Grilled Cheese, 85
Apples
  Apple Mustard, 160
  The Catch Grilled Cheese, 55
Apricot-Jalapeño Relish, 155
Artichokes
  Moroccan Green Olive, Artichoke,
    and Preserved Lemon Spread, 158
  Muffaletta Olive Salad, 157
Asiago cheese
  Asiago, Prosciutto, and Sage Mac,
    136–37
  Basic Mac 'n' Cheese, 120–22
Avocados
  Black Bean and Fresh Corn Grilled
    Cheese, 52–53
  Huevos Rollando Grilled Cheese,
    30–31
  Ultimate California Grilled Cheese,
    45

B

Bacon
  Bacon and Jalapeño Mac, 138–40
  Breakfast-in-Bed Grilled Cheese, 24
  Breakfast Popper Grilled Cheese, 25
  Bro 'Wich Project Grilled Cheese,
    61–63
  Club Turkey Grilled Cheese, 64
  Farmer's Breakfast Grilled Cheese,
    26–27
  Farmyard Club Grilled Cheese, 64
  Grilled Cheese Birthday Cake, 90–92
  Jalapeño Popper Grilled Cheese, 68
  Smoky Lentil Soup, 113
  Tomato-Bacon-Jalapeño Mac Grilled
    Cheese, 44
  Truffled Grilled Cheese with Bacon
    and Chives, 75
Baked Potato Soup, 100–101

Balsamic Onion Marmalade, 161
Basic Mac 'n' Cheese, 120–22
Basil-Lavender Pesto, 159
Basque Sheep Grilled Cheese, 40
BBQ Chicken Mac, 132–33
Beans
  American Chili, 116–17
  Black Bean and Fresh Corn Grilled
    Cheese, 52–53
  Huevos Rollando Grilled Cheese,
    30–31
  Kale and Potato Soup, 99
  White Bean and Ham Soup, 114
Beef
  American Chili, 116–17
  American Dip Grilled Cheese, 85
  Reubenesque Grilled Cheese, 89
  Roast Beef and Blue Cheese Grilled
    Cheese, 83
  St. Patrick's Day Grilled Cheese,
    86–87
  Windy City Grilled Cheese, 84
Bell peppers
  American Chili, 116–17
  Feta Fetish Grilled Cheese, 50–51
  Giardiniera, 149–50
  Kale Slaw, 163
Bel Paese cheese
  Feta Fetish Grilled Cheese, 50–51
Birthday Cake, Grilled Cheese, 90–92
Black Bean and Fresh Corn Grilled
  Cheese, 52–53
Blue cheese
  Basic Mac 'n' Cheese, 120–22
  Foghorn Leghorn Grilled Cheese,
    56–57
  Roast Beef and Blue Cheese Grilled
    Cheese, 83
Bread
  for grilled cheese, 13
  Irish Soda Bread, 88
Bread 'n' Butter Pickles, 147
Breakfast-in-Bed Grilled Cheese, 24

Breakfast Piglet Grilled Cheese, 28
Breakfast Popper Grilled Cheese, 25
Brie cheese
  Sunday Brunch Grilled Cheese,
    32–34
Broccoli-Cheddar Soup, 98
Brown Sugar–Bourbon Sauce, 35
Bro 'Wich Project Grilled Cheese, 61–63
Butter, 13–14
Butternut squash
  Butternut Buster Grilled Cheese,
    76–77
  Butternut Squash Soup, 108–9

C

Cabbage
  Kale Slaw, 163
  St. Patrick's Day Grilled Cheese,
    86–87
Capicola
  Muffaletta Grilled Cheese, 81
Carmody cheese
  Honey Pot Grilled Cheese, 34
  Ultimate California Grilled Cheese,
    45
Carrots
  Giardiniera, 149–50
  Spiced Coconut-Carrot Soup, 110
The Catch Grilled Cheese, 55
Cauliflower
  Curry-Cauliflower Soup, 107
  Giardiniera, 149–50
Celery Purée Soup, 102
Cheddar cheese
  Bacon and Jalapeño Mac, 138–40
  Basic Mac 'n' Cheese, 120–22
  BBQ Chicken Mac, 132–33
  Black Bean and Fresh Corn Grilled
    Cheese, 52–53
  Breakfast-in-Bed Grilled Cheese, 24
  Breakfast Piglet Grilled Cheese, 28
  Broccoli-Cheddar Soup, 98

Bro 'Wich Project Grilled Cheese, 61–63

Chili Mac, 141–43

Classic Breakfast Grilled Cheese, 23

Club Cluck Grilled Cheese, 64

Club Oink Grilled Cheese, 64

Club Turkey Grilled Cheese, 64

Crab Mac, 130–31

Curry-Cauliflower Soup, 107

Farmer's Breakfast Grilled Cheese, 26–27

Farmyard Club Grilled Cheese, 64

Grilled Cheese Birthday Cake, 90–92

Gruyère, Garlic, and White Wine Mac, 124–25

Ham and Herb Mac, 134–35

Mac 'n' Cheese Grilled Cheese, 42–44

Mousetrap Grilled Cheese, 38–39

Piglet Grilled Cheese, 69

St. Patrick's Day Grilled Cheese, 86–87

Cheese, 14–15. *See also individual cheeses*

Chèvre (goat cheese)

Breakfast Popper Grilled Cheese, 25

Chèvre and Fig Chutney Grilled Cheese, 34

Farmyard Club Grilled Cheese, 64

Honey Pot Grilled Cheese, 34

Jalapeño Popper Grilled Cheese, 68

Chicken

BBQ Chicken Mac, 132–33

Club Cluck Grilled Cheese, 64

Foghorn Leghorn Grilled Cheese, 56–57

Indian Leftovers Grilled Cheese, 60

Moroccan Chicken Grilled Cheese, 58–59

Chiles

adjusting heat of, 53

American Chili, 116–17

Apricot-Jalapeño Relish, 155

Bacon and Jalapeño Mac, 138–40

Black Bean and Fresh Corn Grilled Cheese, 52–53

Breakfast Popper Grilled Cheese, 25

Bro 'Wich Project Grilled Cheese, 61–63

Giardiniera, 149–50

Grilled Cheese Birthday Cake, 90–92

handling, 150

Jalapeño Popper Grilled Cheese, 68

Sweet Pickled Jalapeños, 152

Tomato-Bacon-Jalapeño Mac Grilled Cheese, 44

Chili

American Chili, 116–17

Chili Mac, 141–43

Chili Mac Grilled Cheese, 44

Chowder, Fresh Corn, 105

Classic Breakfast Grilled Cheese, 23

Clothes irons, 19

Club Cluck Grilled Cheese, 64

Club Oink Grilled Cheese, 64

Club Turkey Grilled Cheese, 64

Coconut milk

Butternut Squash Soup, 108–9

Spiced Coconut-Carrot Soup, 110

Colby cheese

Bro 'Wich Project Grilled Cheese, 61–63

Club Cluck Grilled Cheese, 64

Club Oink Grilled Cheese, 64

Club Turkey Grilled Cheese, 64

Farmyard Club Grilled Cheese, 64

Mac 'n' Cheese Grilled Cheese, 42–44

Thanksgiving Leftovers Grilled Cheese, 66

Comté cheese

Basic Mac 'n' Cheese, 120–22

Cooking techniques, 16–19

Corn

Black Bean and Fresh Corn Grilled Cheese, 52–53

Fresh Corn Chowder, 105

Corned beef

St. Patrick's Day Grilled Cheese, 86–87

Crab

Crab Mac, 130–31

Crab Mac Grilled Cheese, 44

Cranberry Sauce, 154

Cristo Hispanico Grilled Cheese, 34

Cubano Grilled Cheese, 72–73

Cucumbers

Bread 'n' Butter Pickles, 147

Curry-Cauliflower Soup, 107

D

Don Gondola Grilled Cheese, 78

E

Eggplant

Feta Fetish Grilled Cheese, 50–51

roasting or grilling, 51

Eggs

Breakfast-in-Bed Grilled Cheese, 24

Breakfast Piglet Grilled Cheese, 28

Breakfast Popper Grilled Cheese, 25

Classic Breakfast Grilled Cheese, 23

Farmer's Breakfast Grilled Cheese, 26–27

Green Eggs and Ham Grilled Cheese, 29

Huevos Rollando Grilled Cheese, 30–31

Emmenthaler cheese

Cubano Grilled Cheese, 72–73

Reubenesque Grilled Cheese, 89

F

Farmer's Breakfast Grilled Cheese, 26–27

Farmyard Club Grilled Cheese, 64

Feta Fetish Grilled Cheese, 50–51

Fig Chutney Grilled Cheese, Chèvre and, 34

Fish
    The Catch Grilled Cheese, 55
Foghorn Leghorn Grilled Cheese,
    56–57
Fontina cheese
    Asiago, Prosciutto, and Sage Mac,
    136–37
    Bacon and Jalapeño Mac, 138–40
    Basic Mac 'n' Cheese, 120–22
    Butternut Buster Grilled Cheese,
    76–77
    Crab Mac, 130–31
    Feta Fetish Grilled Cheese, 50–51
    Fontina, Mushroom, and Thyme Mac,
    126–27
    Gruyère, Garlic, and White Wine Mac,
    124–25
    Ham and Herb Mac, 134–35
    Hawaiian Grilled Cheese, 71
    Mac 'n' Cheese Grilled Cheese,
    42–44
    Moscone Grilled Cheese, 48–49
    Mozzarella, Pesto, and Tomato Mac,
    128–29
    Mushroom-Gruyère Grilled Cheese,
    46–47
Fresh Corn Chowder, 105

G

Garlic Jack cheese
    American Dip Grilled Cheese, 85
    Basic Mac 'n' Cheese, 120–22
Giardiniera, 149–50
Goat cheese. *See* Chèvre
Gouda cheese
    Breakfast-in-Bed Grilled Cheese, 24
    The Catch Grilled Cheese, 55
    Mac 'n' Cheese Grilled Cheese,
    42–44
Green Eggs and Ham Grilled Cheese,
    29
Griddles, electric or gas, 17
Grilled cheese (general)
    cooking techniques for, 16–19
    creating new, 15–16
    ingredients for, 12–15

Grilled cheese (recipes)
    American Dip Grilled Cheese, 85
    Basque Sheep Grilled Cheese, 40
    Black Bean and Fresh Corn Grilled
    Cheese, 52–53
    Breakfast-in-Bed Grilled Cheese, 24
    Breakfast Piglet Grilled Cheese, 28
    Breakfast Popper Grilled Cheese, 25
    Bro 'Wich Project Grilled Cheese,
    61–63
    Butternut Buster Grilled Cheese,
    76–77
    The Catch Grilled Cheese, 55
    Chèvre and Fig Chutney Grilled
    Cheese, 34
    Chili Mac Grilled Cheese, 44
    Classic Breakfast Grilled Cheese, 23
    Club Cluck Grilled Cheese, 64
    Club Oink Grilled Cheese, 64
    Club Turkey Grilled Cheese, 64
    Crab Mac Grilled Cheese, 44
    Cristo Hispanico Grilled Cheese, 34
    Cubano Grilled Cheese, 72–73
    Don Gondola Grilled Cheese, 78
    Farmer's Breakfast Grilled Cheese,
    26–27
    Farmyard Club Grilled Cheese, 64
    Feta Fetish Grilled Cheese, 50–51
    Foghorn Leghorn Grilled Cheese,
    56–57
    Green Eggs and Ham Grilled Cheese,
    29
    Grilled Cheese Birthday Cake, 90–92
    Hawaiian Grilled Cheese, 71
    Honey Pot Grilled Cheese, 34
    Huevos Rollando Grilled Cheese,
    30–31
    Indian Leftovers Grilled Cheese, 60
    Jalapeño Popper Grilled Cheese, 68
    Mac 'n' Cheese Grilled Cheese,
    42–44
    Moroccan Chicken Grilled Cheese,
    58–59
    Moscone Grilled Cheese, 48–49
    Mousetrap Grilled Cheese, 38–39
    Muffaletta Grilled Cheese, 81
    Mushroom-Gruyère Grilled Cheese,
    46–47

Piglet Grilled Cheese, 69
    Pizza-wich Grilled Cheese, 79
    Reubenesque Grilled Cheese, 89
    Roast Beef and Blue Cheese Grilled
    Cheese, 83
    St. Patrick's Day Grilled Cheese,
    86–87
    Sunday Brunch Grilled Cheese,
    32–34
    Thanksgiving Leftovers Grilled
    Cheese, 66
    Tomato-Bacon-Jalapeño Mac Grilled
    Cheese, 44
    Truffled Grilled Cheese with Bacon
    and Chives, 75
    Ultimate California Grilled Cheese,
    45
    Wild Turkey Grilled Cheese, 65
    Windy City Grilled Cheese, 84
Gravy, Quick Cream, 67
Gruyère cheese
    Basic Mac 'n' Cheese, 120–22
    Fontina, Mushroom, and Thyme Mac,
    126–27
    Gruyère, Garlic, and White Wine Mac,
    124–25
    Ham and Herb Mac, 134–35
    Mushroom-Gruyère Grilled Cheese,
    46–47
    Reubenesque Grilled Cheese, 89

H

Habanero Jack cheese
    Huevos Rollando Grilled Cheese,
    30–31
Ham. *See also* Prosciutto; Speck
    Breakfast Piglet Grilled Cheese, 28
    Bro 'Wich Project Grilled Cheese,
    61–63
    Club Oink Grilled Cheese, 64
    Cristo Hispanico Grilled Cheese, 34
    Cubano Grilled Cheese, 72–73
    Green Eggs and Ham Grilled Cheese,
    29
    Ham and Herb Mac, 134–35
    Hawaiian Grilled Cheese, 71
    Honey Pot Grilled Cheese, 34
    Piglet Grilled Cheese, 69

White Bean and Ham Soup, 114
Havarti cheese
Bro 'Wich Project Grilled Cheese, 61–63
Club Cluck Grilled Cheese, 64
Club Oink Grilled Cheese, 64
Club Turkey Grilled Cheese, 64
Crab Mac, 130–31
Farmyard Club Grilled Cheese, 64
Foghorn Leghorn Grilled Cheese, 56–57
Mousetrap Grilled Cheese, 38–39
Wild Turkey Grilled Cheese, 65
Hawaiian Grilled Cheese, 71
Herbes de Provence, 41
Herb Jack cheese
American Dip Grilled Cheese, 85
Basic Mac 'n' Cheese, 120–22
Honey Pot Grilled Cheese, 34
Huevos Rollando Grilled Cheese, 30–31

I

Idiazábal cheese
Butternut Buster Grilled Cheese, 76–77
Indian Leftovers Grilled Cheese, 60
Irish Soda Bread, 88

J

Jalapeños. *See* Chiles
Jarlsberg cheese
Muffaletta Grilled Cheese, 81
Reubenesque Grilled Cheese, 89

K

Kalamata Tapenade, 156
Kale
Kale and Potato Soup, 99
Kale Slaw, 163

L

Lemons, Preserved Meyer, 153
Lentil Soup, Smoky, 113
Luscious Mushroom Soup, 103

M

Mac 'n' cheese
Asiago, Prosciutto, and Sage Mac, 136–37
Bacon and Jalapeño Mac, 138–40
Basic Mac 'n' Cheese, 120–22
BBQ Chicken Mac, 132–33
Chili Mac, 141–43
Chili Mac Grilled Cheese, 44
Crab Mac, 130–31
Crab Mac Grilled Cheese, 44
Fontina, Mushroom, and Thyme Mac, 126–27
Gruyère, Garlic, and White Wine Mac, 124–25
Ham and Herb Mac, 134–35
Mac 'n' Cheese Grilled Cheese, 42–44
Mozzarella, Pesto, and Tomato Mac, 128–29
Tomato-Bacon-Jalapeño Mac Grilled Cheese, 44
Mahon cheese
Moroccan Chicken Grilled Cheese, 58–59
Manchego cheese
Cristo Hispanico Grilled Cheese, 34
Marmalade, Balsamic Onion, 161
Meyer Lemons, Preserved, 153
Monterey Jack cheese
Bacon and Jalapeño Mac, 138–40
Basic Mac 'n' Cheese, 120–22
BBQ Chicken Mac, 132–33
Black Bean and Fresh Corn Grilled Cheese, 52–53
Breakfast Popper Grilled Cheese, 25
Chili Mac, 141–43
Chili Mac Grilled Cheese, 44
Classic Breakfast Grilled Cheese, 23
Club Cluck Grilled Cheese, 64
Club Oink Grilled Cheese, 64
Club Turkey Grilled Cheese, 64
Crab Mac Grilled Cheese, 44
Farmyard Club Grilled Cheese, 64
Fontina, Mushroom, and Thyme Mac, 126–27
Grilled Cheese Birthday Cake, 90–92

Jalapeño Popper Grilled Cheese, 68
Mac 'n' Cheese Grilled Cheese, 42–44
Mousetrap Grilled Cheese, 38–39
Tomato-Bacon-Jalapeño Mac Grilled Cheese, 44
Moroccan Chicken Grilled Cheese, 58–59
Moroccan Green Olive, Artichoke, and Preserved Lemon Spread, 158
Mortadella
Muffaletta Grilled Cheese, 81
Moscone Grilled Cheese, 48–49
Mousetrap Grilled Cheese, 38–39
Mozzarella cheese
Basic Mac 'n' Cheese, 120–22
Hawaiian Grilled Cheese, 71
Moscone Grilled Cheese, 48–49
Mozzarella, Pesto, and Tomato Mac, 128–29
Muffaletta Grilled Cheese, 81
Pizza-wich Grilled Cheese, 79
Muenster cheese
Cubano Grilled Cheese, 72–73
Roast Beef and Blue Cheese Grilled Cheese, 83
Muffaletta Grilled Cheese, 81
Muffaletta Olive Salad, 157
Mushrooms
Fontina, Mushroom, and Thyme Mac, 126–27
Luscious Mushroom Soup, 103
Mushroom-Gruyère Grilled Cheese, 46–47
Pulled Pork Stew, 115
Mustard, Apple, 160

O

Oaxaca cheese
Black Bean and Fresh Corn Grilled Cheese, 52–53
Olives
Giardiniera, 149–50
Kalamata Tapenade, 156
Moroccan Green Olive, Artichoke, and Preserved Lemon Spread, 158
Muffaletta Olive Salad, 157

Onions
    Balsamic Onion Marmalade, 161
    Pickled Red Onions, 151
Ossau-Iraty cheese
    Basque Sheep Grilled Cheese, 40
Oven combo method, 18–19

P

Panini presses, 17–18
Pasta. *See* Mac 'n' cheese
Pastrami
    Reubenesque Grilled Cheese, 89
Pea Soup, Split, 111
Pepper Jack cheese
    Huevos Rollando Grilled Cheese, 30–31
    Indian Leftovers Grilled Cheese, 60
Pepperoni
    Pizza-wich Grilled Cheese, 79
Pesto, Basil-Lavender, 159
Pickles
    Bread 'n' Butter Pickles, 147
    Giardiniera, 149–50
    Pickled Red Onions, 151
    Sweet Pickled Jalapeños, 152
Piglet Grilled Cheese, 69
Pineapple
    Hawaiian Grilled Cheese, 71
Pizza-wich Grilled Cheese, 79
Pork. *See also* Bacon; Ham; Sausage
    Cubano Grilled Cheese, 72–73
    Pulled Pork Stew, 115
Potato chips
    BBQ Chicken Mac, 132–33
Potatoes
    American Dip Grilled Cheese, 85
    Baked Potato Soup, 100–101
    Celery Purée Soup, 102
    Farmer's Breakfast Grilled Cheese, 26–27
    Fresh Corn Chowder, 105
    Kale and Potato Soup, 99
    Mushroom-Gruyère Grilled Cheese, 46–47
    Pulled Pork Stew, 115

St. Patrick's Day Grilled Cheese, 86–87
Split Pea Soup, 111
Thanksgiving Leftovers Grilled Cheese, 67
Preserved Meyer Lemons, 153
Prosciutto
    Asiago, Prosciutto, and Sage Mac, 136–37
    Butternut Buster Grilled Cheese, 76–77
    Cristo Hispanico Grilled Cheese, 34
Provolone cheese
    Basic Mac 'n' Cheese, 120–22
    Don Gondola Grilled Cheese, 78
    Muffaletta Grilled Cheese, 81
    Windy City Grilled Cheese, 84
P'tit Basque cheese
    Basque Sheep Grilled Cheese, 40
Pulled Pork Stew, 115

Q

Quick Cream Gravy, 67

R

Ras El Hanout, 59
Relish, Apricot-Jalapeño, 155
Reubenesque Grilled Cheese, 89
Roast Beef and Blue Cheese Grilled Cheese, 83

S

Sage Derby cheese
    Green Eggs and Ham Grilled Cheese, 29
St. Patrick's Day Grilled Cheese, 86–87
Salami
    Don Gondola Grilled Cheese, 78
    Muffaletta Grilled Cheese, 81
Sandwich irons, 19
Sandwich presses, 17–18
San Joaquin Gold cheese
    Ultimate California Grilled Cheese, 45

Sauces
    Basil-Lavender Pesto, 159
    Brown Sugar–Bourbon Sauce, 35
    Cranberry Sauce, 154
    Quick Cream Gravy, 67
Sausage
    Don Gondola Grilled Cheese, 78
    Muffaletta Grilled Cheese, 81
    Pizza-wich Grilled Cheese, 79
Slaw, Kale, 163
Smoky Lentil Soup, 113
Sonoma Jack cheese
    Breakfast Popper Grilled Cheese, 25
    Classic Breakfast Grilled Cheese, 23
Soups
    Baked Potato Soup, 100–101
    Broccoli-Cheddar Soup, 98
    Butternut Squash Soup, 108–9
    Celery Purée Soup, 102
    Curry-Cauliflower Soup, 107
    Fresh Corn Chowder, 105
    Kale and Potato Soup, 99
    Luscious Mushroom Soup, 103
    Smoky Lentil Soup, 113
    Spiced Coconut-Carrot Soup, 110
    Split Pea Soup, 111
    Ten-Minute Tomato Soup, 97
    White Bean and Ham Soup, 114
Speck
    Butternut Buster Grilled Cheese, 76–77
    Cristo Hispanico Grilled Cheese, 34
Spiced Coconut-Carrot Soup, 110
Split Pea Soup, 111
Spreads
    Balsamic Onion Marmalade, 161
    Kalamata Tapenade, 156
    Moroccan Green Olive, Artichoke, and Preserved Lemon Spread, 158
    Muffaletta Olive Salad, 157
Squash. *See* Butternut squash; Zucchini
Stew, Pulled Pork, 115
Stove-top skillet method, 16–17
Strawberries
    Sunday Brunch Grilled Cheese, 32–34

Sweet Pickled Jalapeños, 152
Swiss cheese
    Bro 'Wich Project Grilled Cheese,
      61–63
    Cubano Grilled Cheese, 72–73

T

Tapenade, Kalamata, 156
Ten-Minute Tomato Soup, 97
Thanksgiving Leftovers Grilled Cheese,
  67
Toma cheese
    Ultimate California Grilled Cheese,
      45
Tomatoes
    American Chili, 116–17
    Black Bean and Fresh Corn Grilled
      Cheese, 52–53
    Bro 'Wich Project Grilled Cheese,
      61–63
    The Catch Grilled Cheese, 55
    Club Turkey Grilled Cheese, 64
    Don Gondola Grilled Cheese, 78
    Feta Fetish Grilled Cheese, 50–51
    Hawaiian Grilled Cheese, 71
    Huevos Rollando Grilled Cheese,
      30–31
    Moscone Grilled Cheese, 48–49
    Mozzarella, Pesto, and Tomato Mac,
      128–29
    Muffaletta Grilled Cheese, 81
    Pizza-wich Grilled Cheese, 79
    Smoky Lentil Soup, 113
    Ten-Minute Tomato Soup, 97
    Tomato-Bacon-Jalapeño Mac Grilled
      Cheese, 44
Triple crème cheese
    Sunday Brunch Grilled Cheese,
      32–34
Tuna
    The Catch Grilled Cheese, 55
Turkey
    Bro 'Wich Project Grilled Cheese,
      61–63
    Club Turkey Grilled Cheese, 64
    Farmyard Club Grilled Cheese, 64

    Thanksgiving Leftovers Grilled
      Cheese, 66
    Wild Turkey Grilled Cheese, 65

U

Ultimate California Grilled Cheese, 45

W

Waffle irons, 19
White Bean and Ham Soup, 114
Wild Turkey Grilled Cheese, 66
Windy City Grilled Cheese, 84

Z

Zucchini
    Feta Fetish Grilled Cheese, 50–51
    roasting, 51

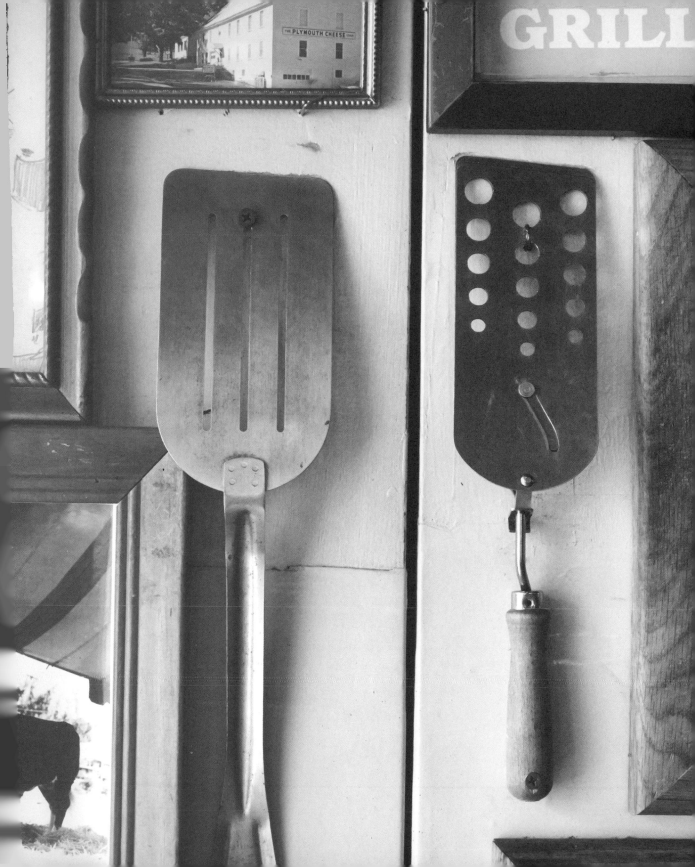

2 FETA, 2 FURIOUS

MY COMPLIMENTS TO THE CHÈVRE!

 Gouda morning to you!

THERE'S A MUENSTER HIDING IN MY FRIDGE

MILLENNIALS, THE FONTINA OF YOUTH

I CAMEMBERT TO WAIT
ANY LONGER FOR
THIS GRILLED CHEESE
TO FINISH COOKING!

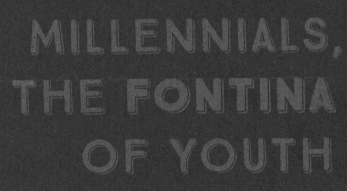

SWEET DRE
WHO AM I
SWEET DRE
SOME OF T

TONIGHT WE'RE GONN